THE RISK OF HOPE

MKLM Library

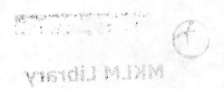

THE RISK OF HOPE

How to Talk about God in the World Today

CARDINAL LUIS ANTONIO TAGLE

ORBIS BOOKS
Maryknoll, New York 10545

Founded in 1970, Orbis Books endeavors to publish works that enlighten the mind, nourish the spirit, and challenge the conscience. The publishing arm of the Maryknoll Fathers and Brothers, Orbis seeks to explore the global dimensions of the Christian faith and mission, to invite dialogue with diverse cultures and religious traditions, and to serve the cause of reconciliation and peace. The books published reflect the views of their authors and do not represent the official position of the Maryknoll Society. To learn more about Maryknoll and Orbis Books, please visit our website at www.maryknollsociety.org.

Copyright © 2018 by Orbis Books

Published by Orbis Books, Box 302, Maryknoll, NY 10545-0302.

Italian edition published as *Il rischio della speranza: Come raccontare Dio ai nostri giorni* © 2016 by EMI, Bologna, Italy.

All rights reserved.

Manufactured in the United States of America

Manuscript editing and typesetting by Joan Weber Laflamme.

Library of Congress Cataloging-in-Publication Data

Names: Tagle, Luis Antonio, author.

Title: The risk of hope : how to talk about God in the world today / Cardinal Luis Antonio Tagle.

Other titles: Original title: Rischio della speranza

Description: Maryknoll : Orbis Books, 2018.

Identifiers: LCCN 2017049806 (print) | LCCN 2018008553 (ebook) | ISBN 9781608337484 (e-book) | ISBN 9781626982826 (pbk.)

Subjects: LCSH: Catholic Church—Doctrines

Classification: LCC BX1751.3 (ebook) | LCC BX1751.3 .T3413 2018 (print) | DDC 30/.2—dc23

LC record available at https://lccn.loc.gov/2017049806

Contents

This Risky Business of Saying "God"

We are at the commencement exercises of a school of theology. But what precisely have you studied? What is this theology? What is it that we taught you in this school? And what is the business of this school as a school of theology?

I was quite struck by an article written by a Canadian Dominican, Jacques Lison, who wrote, "The essential concern of theology is to say 'God.'" This statement struck me because we are so used to hearing that theology is talking *about* God, that it is the *study of* God. But Lison says, "No, the concern of theology, the essential concern of theology, is to say 'God.'" I wonder whether this is what you learned and whether this is what we taught you. Has it been the business of

---

Address delivered at the commencement exercises of Loyola School of Theology, Loyola Heights, Quezon City, March 13, 2002.

Loyola School of Theology (LST), and of other schools of theology, to say "God"?

Theology is not just talking *about* God. It is also doxology. It is a mystical reality. It is recognition. It is contemplation. It is participation in God. But as Saint Paul tells us, "No one can say Jesus is Lord and no one can say '*Abba,* Father' except in the Spirit." Therefore, if theology is about saying "God," then theology must be an action primarily of the Spirit, and of people who will be open to the Spirit so they can say "God."

I want to think that you graduates, including current and future LST students, have heard many ways of saying "God." Not only because every professor of theology espouses a particular theory, uses a certain framework, or has a unique way of saying "God," but also because, in your different courses, you have been initiated into this great tradition of the church—the church handing on its own life. Theology is always at the service of the church.

You must have heard and seen so many ways of saying "God" in the history of the church. I still use much of what I learned from my professors when I was a student here some twenty-five years ago. Only now, there are a few things, here and there, that I also add—new ways of saying "God." Let me indicate a few changes in the history of the church, as indicated in one study by Peter Schineller, SJ.

Who Does Theology?
Who Says "God"?

In the past, seminary professors in their black cassocks—all male—said "God." Later, even university professors could say "God." Then, both males and females could say "God." I saw a photograph of the first student body here at LST, and it had only one woman student in the person of Immaculate Heart of Mary Sister Vicky Palanca. Now, there are new voices that dare to say "God." These new voices express God from their worlds, their experiences, and their concerns; they produce varied ways of saying "God."

Where Was Theology Done?
Where Do You Say "God"?

In the early church, saying "God" was the domain of the bishops—the episcopal setting. Then the monastic setting became the place for saying "God." The great universities and, after Trent, the seminaries became the places to say "God." All of these events occurred mainly in Europe; it was in Europe where they had to say "God." Today, many places are saying "God." In every country "God" can be said. Even in villages and basic ecclesial communities "God" is uttered.

For Whom Do We Do Theology?
For Whom Do We Say "God"?

In the early church we said "God" to convert pagans and heretics so they could see God and follow the true faith. Later, theology was done for future clerics in seminaries. Today we say "God" for victims of society, for the nonpersons, for those who are forgotten. To them we say "God" to assure them there is One who does not forget them. According to David Tracy, now theology addresses many publics, many audiences. You say "God" to the church. You say "God" to the university. You say "God" to society.

With Whom Do We Say "God"?
With Whom Do We Do Theology?

In the past, theology was done with philosophy. Now, it is more interdisciplinary. At all levels, whether within the church in order to understand our tradition and our history better or *ad extra,* we need to say "God" with the human sciences. More important, we have to say "God" in a way that engages the social, economic, political, and cultural realities of people's lives. We say "God" with all of these things.

And How Does One Say "God"?

There was a time when you said "God" by following the Denzinger method. You have a thesis. You know the biblical foundations. You know the teachings of the councils and the popes, and then you add a few things here and there. You have said "God." Then it moved more and more into a historical way of saying "God." Now people engage in what they call critical correlation. Some even engage not only through orthodoxy but also through orthopraxis. Today, we have many different ways of saying "God."

You have been initiated into these varied ways, and this school of theology certainly encourages us to get in touch with this vitality of ways, all at the service of the church, its life and its mission. Part of LST's mission is to prepare men and women to be able to say "God" meaningfully in their worlds and in accordance with their charisms and vocations.

Taking on the Risk in Our Time

We are very sure that what we have offered to you students is not exhaustive, but it is, nevertheless, valuable. Even if you should forget LST or your professors' ways of saying "God," please do not forget to say "God" lest the world forget and believe that God is superfluous. Perhaps more important than remembering the specific ways of saying "God" is to just say "God" with the conviction to engage in this rather risky business of saying "God" in our times. It is not easy to say "God." It is quite risky. Let me offer a few suggestions.

First, in this world of globalization, properly called "elite globalization," Nicanor Perlas notes that this elite globalization is actually a ruthless *growth*. It is also a futureless growth, because it is growth without jobs. It is rootless growth because it is growth that cuts us from the roots of our values and traditions. And it is a meaningless growth because many times people lose their direction in life. In the midst of all these challenges, the world is convincing us to forget our neighbor, to forget God, all in the name of profit and competition. It is not easy to say "God" in a world that wants to forget neighbors. When we forget our neighbors, we will not be able to utter "God." However, we hope that your training here in this school of theology has taught you how to say "God" meaningfully.

As you have learned from us, please also learn to say "God" with the little ones of the world, those whom globalization wants to forget and to deny. Learn from the forgotten ones. Learn from the nonpersons. Allow them to teach you how to say "God."

On the first Sunday after my ordination as bishop, the *Simbang Gabi*—the novena masses attended at dawn by Filipinos in preparation for Christmas—had already begun. After celebrating the Eucharist in the cathedral and still wearing my full episcopal regalia, I greeted the people as they went out the door. As I stood there, I saw little children who were selling flowers impeding the progress of the people leaving the church. I ran after them, scolding them until we reached the road. I was still in my full regalia as I was shouting at those children. I told them, "Look, we have not forbidden you to sell flowers, but let us put some order here! You can sell flowers here at the gate. The people who are attending mass and the people who are leaving the church will certainly pass through the gate."

The children were all trembling before me. I looked at them and I spotted the tallest girl and I asked her, "You! How old are you?" She said, "Fourteen." I replied, "You see! You're fourteen years old. Is it difficult to understand what I'm saying? That you can sell at this point and not beyond it?" And she answered, "No, I can understand."

Then I looked at the smallest boy, a very dirty looking boy. I said, "You! How old are you?" He looked up, smiled, and said, "Seven." I said, "You're seven years old. Can you understand what I'm saying?" It was then that he hugged me. He was so small that his hands only reached my waist. He hugged me and again smiled the sweetest smile. He gently said, "Father, you are now a bishop." I stopped, and I said, "Yes." God was calling me again and asking me to utter "God" to these children in compassion.

I have never experienced selling flowers. I have never wanted for anything; as a child, all I had to do was go to school. These children had to work every Sunday to have something. There I was, uttering laws, policies, order, and cleanliness. And this young boy uttered a word addressed to my heart, to my identity.

For the next half hour I just stayed with the children at the gate, still in my full episcopal regalia, and had a grand time talking with them. After a few days of being ordained bishop, those children taught me how to listen to God and how to say "God."

Last Saturday I was invited to bless a chapel in Mendez, Cavite, where I was first assigned as a young priest and pastor. Father Reddy Corpuz said maybe we could use the occasion for a pastoral visit. Not the formal pastoral visit where the bishop looks at the books and the accounts, but just a visit. So I said, "Yes, sure." It was also an occasion for me to see my former parishioners.

When I arrived at the site of the new chapel, all the bands were playing, and I was given a big, big key to the town. As I entered the chapel, I saw the elderly woman who used to take care of us in 1982. After mass she would serve us coffee and *pan de sal*. I approached her and I said, "Grandmother Juana! You are still alive!" She grabbed my hand and said, "You still remember me. You still know my name." Then she said, "I'm dying of cancer. I have not been home here for years. Now I live in Manila to be close to the hospital but when I learned that you were coming here as a bishop, I forced my nieces and nephews to take me." She added, "It was worth it. It was worth the travel and all the pain. You still know me. You still know my name." Still holding my hand, she put it near her breast and said, "Pray to God. Pray that I may be healed." But within me I was protesting, "I cannot heal you. I cannot." Yet she was looking at me in total faith, believing that somehow, through this thin bishop, God would heal her.

At the end of the mass I could not leave the chapel. People were crowding around me—in front of me, behind me, to my left, my right, even above me. I was afraid people would be under me! True enough, I saw a little boy trapped there. I pleaded with the people, "Please give this small boy enough space." Then an elderly woman said, "We apologize, Bishop! But you are the first bishop I have seen, and I will probably not see

a bishop again in my life. Please don't deny me this opportunity."

In these ways people say "God." Very simple. And I
could not believe it.

Theology says the bishop possesses the fullness of
the sacred. At the recently concluded Synod of Bishops
on Bishops, the theme that kept recurring was, "The
bishop is the *apparitio Dei* [apparition of God]. The
bishop is the *visitatio Dei* [visitation of God]." It is, as it
were, asking people to look at me, to focus on me. I
will never teach that in my class! I will have to resign
first before I ever include that in my course! But I also
need to listen to how people say "God"—they say it by
patting your back or clutching your hand. They say it by
telling you: "You are now a bishop," or "This is a unique
experience, and it may not be repeated."

Rather, learn from the people, the forgotten ones,
your neighbors. Remember that *our* way of saying
"God" is not the *only* way. Learn from them. Learn
from the victims of senseless violence and suffering.
Learn how they say "God" in hope. Learn from those
pushed to the limits of the paradox of saying "God,"
who sometimes leave it unsaid but never forget God.
Learn from them.

For several days now I have been reading the letters of Father Pavel Florenski, a Russian Orthodox
priest, mathematician, philosopher, artist, theologian,

patriarch, and martyr. He was imprisoned for a long time at a gulag and died in Leningrad on December 8, 1937. One of the most precious gifts I received at ordination was a collection of his letters to his wife and family. In his letters I think Father Pavel is saying "God" in the name of many victims of society. Let me end this sharing by quoting a few lines from his letters.

On October 3, 1933, he wrote to his wife: "I always think of you, and I live only by this. I am extremely worried for not having received from you even a line. I don't know how and by what means you live. How is the health of your mother? How is my own mother? Do the children still remember me? Or are they beginning to forget me?" This is a prayer. Someone who knows he will lose his life but, for one last moment, says "God" by saying, "Don't forget me."

On May 13, 1937, he wrote to his wife: "I kiss you with affection. Find time to rest this summer. Take a walk often, if not in the forest at least in the open field. Take a walk especially in the afternoon, when the sun is low, and remember me."

"Remember me," a way of saying "God." "I'm alone. I feel abandoned, but God, don't forget me." This reminds us of that great person who said "God" all his life and those who heard him were offended. He uttered "God" in love and called him *Abba*. He uttered "God" in pain: "Why have you abandoned me?" He said "God" in hope: "Into your hands I commend my spirit." He uttered "God" in the silence of death and in the rising to life in the Father's bosom. He is the one who really teaches us how to say "God."

Now, dear graduates, continue saying "God" with all the joys and pains and risks it involves. Continue saying "God" with all the praise and lament it invites. Continue saying "God" with all the silence that that mystery creates and evokes. Continue . . .

2

At the Well in Sychar

Priestly Formation
and the New Evangelization

I would like to share some thoughts with you about formation. What does that word really mean? What does it mean to form someone, or to help someone be formed toward being something or someone? In the extraordinary synod of bishops, which recently concluded, there was one bishop who said, "We have nine to ten years to form priests, to prepare seminarians to become priests. And after that long process we're not even sure if they'll become good priests." Then, he asked, "What formation do we give to persons who

---

Adapted from a talk delivered at the seminar Proclaiming the Joy of the Gospel as Renewed Evangelizers in Asia, organized by the Federation of Asian Bishops' Conferences (FABC), in Pattaya, Thailand, November 10–15, 2014.

are preparing for marriage?" He was insinuating that if there is no formation, why are we surprised that some marriages fail? So, he challenges the church. We want the marriage to succeed. But what formation are we giving? Still again, the problem of formation. What does this mean?

Pope Benedict, in one of his last meetings with some bishops, asked us, "In your countries, who or what are the main shapers of culture? They are the ones who form our young people." Identify who or what are the main movers or shapers of culture. Maybe we can learn from them. They are the ones who are forming, or, as we may say, deforming young people. They have the secret formula for how to influence minds and hearts. Especially young people. They are being influenced without their even realizing that their mentalities are already being changed, that their value systems are already being transformed. For example, see how powerful media and social communications are in forming hearts and minds.

We have to review and assess the whole area of formation. We even need to ask painful questions: Are our seminary structures really "formative"? What type of priests do they form?

I would like to look at the message issued by the Synod of Bishops on the new evangelization in 2012. The message used the biblical narrative of the encounter between Jesus and the woman of Samaria at Jacob's well, in Sychar. This simple narrative could provide for us a framework for understanding what we call the new evangelization. At least it offers an orientation pertinent to our concern, the formation of future priests.

We know the story in John 4. Jesus was journeying with his disciples. He stops by the well. The woman arrives. Jesus asks for a drink, and the woman reacts. Then that starts a whole conversation about water, which then turns to living water. Then it shifts to "call your husband." There was no husband to talk about. Then, the question, "Who are you? Are you a prophet?" Then from prophet, Jesus is revealed as the Messiah. The woman forgets her water jar, the main reason for her coming to the well. She runs to the people of her town. She's an evangelizer now.

Look at how Jesus formed her—at the well. Not at the school of theology. At the well. Formation happens there. This zealous woman runs around the town telling people, "I have met the Messiah." And the people begged Jesus to stay, and he obliged. He stayed for two more days. And at the end the people told the woman, "At first we believed that he was the Messiah on the strength of your word. But now we believe because we have heard him, we have seen him, we have encountered him." And those people probably would have spread the good news. A very simple story, which we all know.

But the Synod of Bishops says, let us dwell on this story and let it provide the matrix for some key ideas regarding the new evangelization. I have here five points that I will relate to formation.

Jesus Is a Traveler

Jesus was on a journey with his disciples. He is described as weary, tired, and thirsty. Jesus, the one sent by God, the Son of God, the Word made flesh, is depicted as an ordinary traveler. He experiences the weariness of many other brothers and sisters as they journey through life. And this is significant—Jesus gets to the well before the woman gets there. It is as though he is really waiting for the woman to come, as though he sits there to welcome the woman.

Now this image of Jesus as a traveler, as someone who experiences the burdens, the difficulties of traveling, presents a powerful image of someone or of a community with a mission. God's chosen evangelizer is not coming in a triumphant mode but as an ordinary traveler. This is a far cry from the image of an evangelizer as a triumphant conqueror.

The synod invites us to learn from Jesus. Why not travel as a companion with people? This is not a new idea. This is the spirit of *Gaudium et spes*: "The hopes and joys, the sorrows and anxieties of the men and women of our time, especially of the poor and those in any way afflicted, are the same hopes and joys, sorrows and anxieties of the followers of Christ." Vatican II says this is the way of all followers of Christ. And maybe we can add: Especially the ordained, whose preeminent ministry is to evangelize—to evangelize by traveling with people

I want to relate this to the question of formation. Formation is about walking with people. In many cultures becoming a seminarian involves a step up from the rest of humanity. Becoming a deacon is two steps above the rest of humanity. Becoming a priest? Wow! You belong more to heaven than to earth. You are perceived as a journeyer with the angels and not as a traveler with human beings. You become a bishop. Wow! Imagine what happens to us when we become cardinals!

But I tell you that when I was a deacon, going to villages to conduct Bible services with communion—no sacristan, no altar accompanied me. I was just a deacon. When I got ordained as a priest, so many of these young children would volunteer to accompany me because they hoped to get a free breakfast or a free lunch. If you're attached to a priest, you expect to experience and taste the fringe benefits of being close to a priest. Now that I am a cardinal, so many people claim to be my relatives! Everyone wants to be associated with us. And if we are not careful, such cultural mores will form us to be journeyers not with the people, but with our own.

Being with People

How do we instill this in our seminarians? We need to look closely at the culture of the seminarians. Are we giving the wrong signals? Are we making the seminarians believe that they are a caste above the rest? After ordination they become untouchable. This is the career mentality that the recent popes have been decrying. Let us look at our language. Maybe part of the problem lies in our constantly telling our seminarians, "You are the chosen ones!" This implies that the rest are not chosen. And so the seminarians feel special. "We are chosen." And when they see a lay person, they say: "Poor, poor person. Not chosen by God. . . . And *I* am one of the few chosen. Lord, thank you that I am not like the rest." Then we produce Pharisees and hypocrites.

Formation in solidarity means feeling one with people, understanding their tiredness, understanding their confusion because we also get confused, understanding their suffering because we also suffer. It involves developing compassion rather than a judgmental attitude. This is the life in community, this is the life in the apostolate that we need to instill. Let us review the whole culture in the seminary, the diocese, the ecclesiastical culture. Are our cultures formative of travelers, companions on the journey with the poor and weary?

A Traveler in Hostile Territory

So Jesus is a traveler. But let us now focus on the place where he travels. Saint John identifies the town of Sychar as being in Samaritan territory. So this was enemy territory. We know that the Jews and the Samaritans had very little in common. Jesus does not avoid hostile territory. The synod reminds us that many aspects of our contemporary world are really quite hostile toward Christian faith. Nevertheless, this world is still God's creation. So, how do we engage this world, not only looking at its problems, but also at the signs of hope, the signs of God's presence in that world? For despite its weakness, it remains God's world. It is the world where the Son of God became incarnate. It is a world where the Son of God ministered, where he died. It is also in this world that the Son of God rose from the dead. It is in this world, and not in another world, where the church was born, and where the Spirit blew, and continues to blow.

The new evangelization does not make us blind to problems. But how come, sometimes, we see the problems clearly but are blind to signs of God's presence? Thus, we are blind to the opportunities that this broken world offers us for evangelization. For example, in some parts of the world we lament the rise of secularization. "Oh, it is hostile to religion." But during the synod, it emerged that there are countries where one religion wants to take over, one religion is imposed on all, and what they say is: "What we need is a secular state; not a theocratic state." Secularity also has its contribution. Many Christians are persecuted because they do not live in secular states.

Jesus enters enemy territory, stays there, and seizes the opportunity to produce evangelizers. Pope Francis has been telling us that he does not want a church that is pure because it has avoided any wounds or scars. How do we develop in seminaries the discerning capacity to see the presence of God's spirit, the opportunities? In Asia this is very akin to the dialogical approach, whereby we see the seeds of the presence of the Spirit, of values, of truth in people, religion, and cultures that differ from us, and learn how to take advantage of opportunities.

Mutuality

Jesus begs the Samaritan woman for water. He begs. A Jew asks a Samaritan woman and that disturbs her. This opens a conversation, a dialogue in which Jesus speaks about living water, and presents himself as the giver of living water. Now the roles are reversed. The woman begs Jesus for that water. At the beginning it is Jesus who is begging, and the woman is the giver. Toward the end of the story it is the woman who is begging, and it is Jesus who is giving water. Now this is important in the new evangelization; Jesus and the woman are both beggars and givers. The new evangelization demands this mutuality. The synod of bishops, reflecting on this story, challenges us to be a listening, welcoming community, especially to the lost, the abandoned, the neglected, learning from them, even begging them to give us water, to give us wisdom. Part of formation is to engage in self-examination. We have a lot to give. Are we givers who pretend that we have all the answers, and that we cannot learn any more from others? Are we operating from that standpoint that the rest of the world will receive from us, but we have nothing to gain from others?

We need an attitude of mutuality, which comes with humility. In the early stages of seminary formation I hope that those in charge of the seminarians will check whether they are learning in the seminary this humble art of listening and learning. When I was still teaching, I made my students read stories at the beginning of the semester. Difficult stories about hunger, murder, rape, and so on. And then I asked the questions: How do you talk to people about grace in such situations? How do you talk about the love of God?

What I tried to impress on them was the importance of learning how to control their tongues. We are too quick to explain without first listening to the cries of the people. Sometimes the best response is silence: compassionate silence. The people may experience Jesus more through our listening than through our words.

My point was verified by a student who said, "I went to the wake of a young girl who had died." There he encountered the girl's mother. He asked her how the girl died and learned that she had been sick for a number of months. Being a triumphant seminarian, and knowing all the answers, he told the mother, "Well, God is good. He has given your daughter rest. Your daughter is now at peace." And the mother said, "God gave my daughter rest. But does God see the pain of a mother who has lost her daughter? Does God see that?"

So, I asked the seminarian: "What did you do?"

He said, "I left the wake."

There was an opportunity to learn something there: to shut up. The church thinks that it is evangelizing by a multiplication of words. There is a compulsion to say something about everything! God speaks, but God also listens. Mutuality.

I encourage you to read the recent document from the International Theological Commission on the Sensus Fidei. One practical application of that is that "we need to listen to the lay people, especially of the poor. They have a spiritual instinct about the Gospel that the learned probably do not possess." The document cites the words of Jesus: "I praise you, Father, for hiding these from the learned and the wise and revealing them to the little ones."

Speaking the Truth in Love

Jesus tells the Samaritan woman to call her husband, and she claims that she does not have one. And Jesus tells her the truth about her and her relationships. She has had five husbands. This leads her to suspect that this Jewish man is a prophet, even the Messiah, who will announce all things to us: "You have told about everything that I have done." And Jesus talks about worship in truth and in spirit, and admits to her, "Yes, I am he." This is an important element of the new evangelization—speaking the truth with respect and love.

Jesus here is an evangelizer, the bearer of truth. He tells the truth about this woman. In a way, if we use some current terminology, this Jesus *names* the woman, names her for who she truly is. Probably this woman has been hiding her true identity. But one Bible scholar in Rome during the synod said: "Why do we presume that this woman is sinful, just because she has had five husbands? She might be a widow, a widow being given to brothers. Why do we always depict her as a sinner?" Thanks be to God that we have such exegetes who open to us new possibilities.

Evangelization is about naming people, leading them to experience the truth about themselves. And in embracing the truth about themselves, they detect the presence of God. "Are you the prophet? Are you the Messiah?" So the new evangelization does not mean abandoning the truth, but rather knowing the people to whom the truth is to be proclaimed, and doing it in charity, and with respect. Probably this woman, if she was a sinner, was mesmerized by the respect that she got from this Jewish man.

So let us review our intellectual formation both in seminary and in the ongoing formation of priests. Pope Francis has been attacking the creeping Phariseeism in the church. In fact, Pope Benedict already did that during his pontificate. Pope Benedict, in some of his discourses, said, "You don't call that person an evangelizer. You call that person a hypocrite. You don't call that person a bearer of good news, you call that person a Pharisee." Truth with love. Let us review our formation with this in mind.

Religious Experience

Finally, the woman, after this encounter with Jesus, went into the city and became an evangelizer. The other people of the city were brought to Jesus. She leaves behind her water jar. Probably her deepest thirst was already quenched. She was there not simply for water but for truth. She was there for truth; she was there to see God; she was there to see herself. She was there for truth and love. And that was her deepest thirst. It was quenched by Jesus. There was no more need for the jar. And so she goes.

As the First Letter of John states: "What we have seen with our eyes, what we have heard regarding the word of life, we in turn proclaim to you." This is the experience of the Samaritan woman. She has heard, she has touched, she has seen, and there is no containing her. "Never mind the water jar. I have to go. I have to tell people. I have met the Messiah." The content of evangelization is the Messiah. But not just any kind of Jesus; the Jesus she has talked to, the Jesus who has loved her, the Jesus who has made her face the truth about herself and the truth about God.

The new evangelization, of course, will include new methods, techniques, strategies, and so forth. But let us not forget that the task of evangelization and the challenge of forming evangelizers—whether seminarians or priests—come from a religious experience. Let us learn from Jesus and the woman. What made the woman an evangelizer? An experience of Jesus! A religious experience, a gripping, a life-changing experience.

In the seminaries, in our day-to-day pastoral work, do we pay attention to that space for encountering Jesus? That space that will change us and will fire us up again to become bearers of good news? Sometimes our formation in the seminaries and our ongoing formation may be too academic, and lately we focus on strategies and skills. They are all important. But as the story tells us, what really forms an evangelizer is a gripping experience of Jesus—a religious experience that makes us committed to the good news. Do our spiritual directors and our formation programs focus only on techniques and on content? How about helping people, identify experiences of Jesus in their lives—experiences that will transform them into committed evangelizers?

3

Opening Hearts

Insights from *Evangelii gaudium*

The Formation of the Person of the Evangelizer

Evangelization is a highly personal matter. It is vital that we take a look at how evangelizers are formed. We do not want seminarians or priests who know the content of faith very well, are walking encyclopedias, speak many languages, and are well versed in pastoral strategies, but who personally suffer from a dearth of humanity.

When I visit parishes, especially during their anniversaries and all of the pastors are present, I can sense

---

Adapted from the second part of an address delivered at the seminar Proclaiming the Joy of the Gospel as Renewed Evangelizers in Asia, organized by the Federation of Asian Bishops' Conferences (FABC), in Pattaya, Thailand, November 10–15, 2014.

who among them has developed a loving relationship with the people. Not all of them, I assure you! Some are very well remembered as good builders, and others for their financial expertise. All these are important, but there is a question of who among them was able to develop a loving relationship with people.

This matters a lot, and Pope Francis is asking us to return to this question. We must address this question right at its roots, in the formation of the person of the evangelizer. Some may speak of authenticity; others call it integrity. But authentic persons—persons of integrity—capture the attention of people. Such persons attract interest, not necessarily because of the words they utter, but sometimes with their simple presence, the quality of their person. If the person is authentically Christian, if he is a person of integrity—meaning, there is no dichotomy between his ordinary life and the spirit of the gospel—he will shine forth.

The Homily and Humility

The Holy Father has expressed his concern for the homily in terms that are very spiritual. The homilist is a listener to the word: approaching the word of God as his own, making it part of his person by a deep listening, a listening entails conversion, because he has allowed the word of God to enter him. The Holy Father adds that it is not enough to listen to the word of God; there is also a need to listen to the people's context, their life situation. Before doing the talking in a homily, there is first a lot of listening needed.

I am appealing to those who are teaching homiletics. Sometimes we turn the course into a world of techniques and sophistication. Some even ask their seminarians to do a video recording of themselves for a critique by their classmates. "You move your head very often." "You stick out your tongue." And so forth. Avoid these! Look to the left, then to the right and then start! While presentation techniques are important, remember that the person is to proclaim the word of God—better still, to comment on the life of the people in the light of the word of God. That is the description of the homily. We are not exegetically commenting on the word of God; we are commenting on the life of the people in the light of the word of God. For that to happen, the person of the homilist must do a lot of listening.

Aside from the techniques, those assigned in training the seminarians and priests for homiletics must be attentive to that. They should sense whether the seminarians have listened to the word of God, whether they have appropriated it, and whether they have immersed themselves in the life of the people. When I was still a rector, I saw a seminarian in the middle of the night preparing for his homiletics class. I said, "What will you preach on in your class on the annunciation?"

He said: "Do you have time, Father? I will show you. After proclaiming the Gospel, I will disappear, then show up again with wings. I will wear a pair of wings and tell the people I am the angel Gabriel."

I told him: "Look, if you are assigned in the cathedral where there are masses one hour after another, you do not have time to change costumes. The homily is not about costumes. Besides, you do not look like an angel, and you definitely don't look like the Blessed Mother."

The point of the homily is to enkindle a fire in the hearts of the people, just as happened to the Samaritan woman at the well: "Yes, that is true. He was speaking to me!" This requires a lot of listening and also study. Some priests take their stories from movies and tele-novelas. Better to rely on person-to-person encounters. Visit people in their homes; go to the slums and take your stories from the people.

An Evangelizing Church That Embraces Everyone

The Holy Father is encouraging us to be an evangeliz-ing church that embraces everyone, that is inclusive, especially when it comes to the poor and vulnerable, the ones that society already excludes. The preference for the poor is not a political or social choice for the church. According to *Evangelii gaudium* it is a theological choice, meaning, this is the way of God. It is not a passing sign. It is the way of the *Theos*—the way of God who loved the poor and became poor in Jesus so that we may become rich in the full light of sharing in God's life. This inclusive approach, especially with its preference for the poor and the vulnerable, includes with it a critique of prevailing mindsets, systems, and lifestyles that set aside the poor.

On this point, formation in the seminary must be very clear. I remember a seminarian approaching me in the 1990s, saying: "Father, our rooms are so small. I noticed that they were built in the 1970s during the time of dictatorship. But now time has changed. The rooms are very small. Can we knock down some of the walls to make one room of two?"

I said: "Wait, is your room small, or have you accumulated a lot of things? If you have only two shirts, then the cabinet is big. If you have only one pair of shoes, the shoe rack is big. Now what really is the problem? Is it the room or your things?"

"Oh, Father, I am just joking," said the seminarian, because he knew I already knew the answer.

In the seminary, stewardship must be taught. Otherwise we produce priests who in their seminary days started talking of "my room" and now as priests say "my parish." They cannot be transferred anymore because they do not have a sense of mission, only proprietorship and entitlement. Where did it begin? In the seminary, with "mine!"

A concrete expression of this, according to the Holy Father, is the role of popular piety. Popular piety in the church is a vital and important area of evangelization. In popular piety we have a culture, the gospel, the Spirit of God, and the poor knitted together in a mysterious way. In many parts of the world this popular piety is the bearer of faith transmitted from one generation to the next by simple means. Of course, there is a lot to be purified and evangelized in popular piety. But in churches where popular piety has been thrown out of the window and only formal catechism, formal theological classes, and formal religious education are retained, the faith is now in decline.

May I please ask this august body of bishops and formators, do we introduce our seminarians to the popular religious experience of our people? Or are they so divorced from popular piety that when they become priests they will question the people: "Why are you so superstitious?" It is also good for us pastors to lead some of the novenas and to be present with the people. When they see that we are one with them, the purification that we need to introduce will come easier because they know that we understand them and we are coming from where they are at.

Temptation to Pastoral Workers

Finally, there is a need, according to the Holy Father, to identify the temptations facing pastoral workers. We all experience such temptations (see *Evangelii gaudium*, nos. 76–109). The pope mentioned things like selfishness and spiritual laziness. This is manifested in the attitude, "I already spent nine years studying the Bible, so I do not see a need to deepen my knowledge of it. I do not need to prepare my homilies anymore because I have already preached them before." There are even some who are clever in keeping the outlines of their homilies. When they have completed cycles A, B, and C, and it is time to peach on Cycle A again, they simply say: "Ah, yes, I know this! No more need to pray and reflect. I already preached about this before!" Spiritual laziness!

With these, I usually crack a joke with people on the need for the transfer of priests. I say, "We need to transfer them every three years because the people have already heard them preach on Cycles A, B, and C. So they will not hear again, it is better to transfer them!"

Another temptation is pessimism. Pope John XXIII said at the opening of Vatican II: "There are so many prophets of gloom and doom. They talk only of negative things." He said, "I disagree with them." As Pope Francis comments: "There are some Christians who look like they have just come out from a funeral—pessimists—no joy, no hope! To these we proclaim: 'Jesus is risen!'"

Spiritual worldliness is the other temptation. This is a matter of using spiritual matters for worldly gain. Spiritual worldliness, what a term—though it is not something new. It has been a temptation to many people in the church since time immemorial. Say, for example, a woman gives you an envelope and says, "Father, please pray for my daughter who is taking a very important exam. She wants to enter a university. Please pray for her."

Then you take the envelope with her contribution. But do you pray?

After a few months you happen to see the woman again, and she says, "Father, thank you for your prayers."

And you start to recall, "Oh yes, is your son well now? Has he got out of the hospital?"

Then the woman will say, "It is my daughter for whom I asked you to pray."

And you say to save yourself from shame," Oh, yes! Yes, I prayed for her."

Oh, come on! That is why I warn people not to ask us to pray for their intentions, because many times we do not pray! Now, if you want to accept donations, pray! Take it seriously! Do not use your role in the church to amass wealth.

Finally, the Holy Father says we are warring among ourselves. This has come up in many ways in his speeches and talks at audiences in Rome. There is always bickering, fighting among the priests and the bishops, the lay people among themselves, the lay people and the priests. There is a lot of gossip, a lot of bickering. . . . Precious time is lost to useless in-fighting, especially when it comes to ecclesiastical politics. "Why was he the one appointed to the cathedral when I have a doctorate and he doesn't have one?"

All of these things point to the community in the seminary so that seminarians are trained to live with one another and don't spend precious time on trivial things. Let me end with this: The person who internalizes the word of God can embrace the poor and the vulnerable. Such a person is strong enough and authentic enough to resist these pastoral temptations that block evangelization. The church is not alone in looking for authenticity. But this is our contribution: authentic persons bearing the gospel with joy. This is the missionary joy that comes when God sends a person to the peripheries, to the vulnerable, to the forgotten. This joy is something an authentic evangelizer will manifest, even without words.

4

Transformed into an Apostle

I would like to attempt to do a fresh reading of what people have been saying regarding mission. The theology of mission that I would like to present does not wish to explain again the why and how of mission, but rather to indicate a few points coming from the grace of the moment. Hopefully, the missionary calling and fervor are reawakened in every baptized Catholic in the Philippines as we anticipate the coming National Mission Congress. The congress is being held during the Great Jubilee of Redemption, the Great Jubilee of the Year 2000. It is significant and not a mere coincidence that we will have this National Mission Congress as we commemorate the Jubilee of the Incarnation. The incarnation of the Word of God should lead us in understanding mission.

Adapted from a lecture delivered during Theological Hour at Loyola School of Theology, Loyola Heights, Quezon City, September 20, 2000.

There are many doors through which we can enter to understand mission. What does the incarnation of the Word of God tell us regarding mission? If we enter this particular door of the incarnation, what type of mission or understanding of mission will be opened up to us? Let me focus on three points.

The Incarnation as a Principle of Mission

In Galatians 4:4, Paul says, "When the fullness of time came, the Father sent his son born of a woman." Very simply put, but very dense. In its simplicity of formulation, it strikes the heart. The incarnation of the Word of God as planned by the Father is the fullness of time, of history, and of human existence. This taking flesh through a woman is the fullness of time that conquers the emptiness of life, of time, and of human existence. This fullness of time coincides with the incarnation. But what is in the incarnation that makes it an experience of the fullness of time?

The incarnation of the Word of God is also the fullness of God's self-communication. It is the fullness of God's self-disclosure in love. Such is the reason why even in your ordinary daily life a feeling of emptiness may already be an indication that self-communication in love is not happening. When you are with a loved one and both of you freely show your inner selves and accept each other's full disclosure, time stops because time is full. When you look at your watch, you wonder, "We've been talking already for five hours, and we did not notice it." Time is so full. But when you are in the classroom listening to your teacher and there is no fullness of communication, time becomes empty. You are bored and wonder, "When will this end?" Then you fall asleep.

The incarnation is the fullness of God's manifestation of love in human form bringing with it the fullness of time. The incarnation is making God known in a full way, in a way that is not to be compared with Moses's making God known, with Elijah's making God known. No matter how great these people were, nothing can compare with the fullness of God's manifestation of Self in the Incarnate Word.

Galatians 4:4 is to be read with Colossians 1:15. After a long description of who Jesus is, Paul says that this Jesus, this Son of God, is the image of the invisible God. This text reflects one of the deepest longings of humanity. We want to see God. Nowadays, people want not only to see God, but they also want us to point to where God is. This question is just one of the many painful questions of people who are victims of society, victims of war in Mindanao, victims of rape, and even those who are victims of their wealth but find their lives empty. At one point they ask, "What is the face of God? Where is God?"

This is not a new question. In John 14, Philip himself asks Jesus, "Master, show us the Father and we shall be satisfied." If we see God, then we will no longer want for anything. If we see God, we will find the satisfaction of our hearts and the satisfaction of life. But Jesus was quite peeved when he said, "Philip, how come I have been with you and you still do not know me? He who sees me, sees the Father." This Jewish person, a seemingly ordinary human being called Jesus, is actually the image of God. So when people want to see God, we can always tell them, "You want to see God? Go to Jesus. He is the image of God."

If you take Galatians 4 and Colossians 1:15 and use them as guides to understand what the incarnation is, then you will find that the incarnation is simply making God known and seen so that the hearts of people, like Philip's heart, will be satisfied. When the deepest longings of our hearts find fulfillment, the fullness of time and of life is experienced.

Therefore, to describe mission within the horizon of the incarnation means using Jesus and his incarnation as the paradigm of mission itself; mission is making God, making the Father, known and seen as the fullness of love by being fully human the way Jesus was fully human.

Some Characteristics of the Mission of Jesus

How was this basic principle of the incarnation as the manifestation of God's love in a fully human form manifested in Jesus? It is to be hoped that by exploring this principle we will also be given some signposts for understanding the challenge of mission for us during this Jubilee Year of the Incarnation. There are many, but let me indicate three important things regarding the mission of Jesus arising from principle of the incarnation.

God Is Involved in Human History

The incarnation is not just God becoming flesh or becoming human. In fact, when we look at the life of Jesus and his ministry, the incarnation shows the depths of God's involvement in human history and human affairs. The incarnation is not just about *being* human. There are many human beings, but they do not get involved in human history. Just having flesh and blood does not automatically mean I am involved.

The incarnation as a mission paradigm does not mean that Jesus simply assumes the human body. The assumption of the human body for Jesus meant that God was really getting himself messed up. He became entangled in this mess called human existence.

Jesus's identification and solidarity with the human condition—its problems, longings, sufferings, failures, dreams, and hopes—is a missionary element of the incarnation. This, I think, is the root of what we call incarnation. The incarnation of Jesus is a mission of getting involved. We have to get involved in human things.

Gustavo Gutiérrez says that mission is not to be tied only to a geographic space. For example, the men and women of the Philippine church are constantly challenged to be missionaries in Asia. But Asia is not just a geographic space where you can say, "I've been to Bangkok. I was in Hong Kong. I was in China." If you do, then you were merely a tourist, not a missionary! Gutiérrez rightly notes that mission must tie Christians, just like Jesus, to *human* space, because that is the very principle of the incarnation. This is the reason why in *Ecclesia in Asia* the Holy Father and the bishops of Asia depicted Asia not only in terms of place, but also in terms of the longings, thirst, hunger, dreams, values, history, and heritage of a people. If the Philippine church wants to follow the mission of Jesus, it must operate from the perspective of revealing a God-in-this-world, for many people feel that God does not care, that God is silent, that God has abandoned human beings.

A few weeks ago a beggar appeared at the door of our seminary in Tagaytay. The man was very dirty, and

he carried a baby sucking from a bottle of what looked
like dirty water, brownish water. You knew the baby
was very hungry from the way it sucked at the bottle
with full force. It was so innocent that it probably did
not know the difference between milk and dirty water.
The man stood outside my window, and I asked where
he was from. He said, "I'm here from Payatas. We lost
our house." He came to Tagaytay to look for his siblings,
but he did not know where they were living.

I asked him, "Do you want to eat?"

"I want to eat," he said, and then he asked me, "Are
you a priest?"

I said, "Yes."

"Father, where is God?"

I did not know how to answer him. I tried to avoid
the question and told him, "Somebody will come with
your food."

My encounter with that man was an invitation to
mission. Can I get involved? Can I cross that window
that divides me from a victim? Can I leave my room and
somehow, even just for a few minutes, get involved?
I may not be able to solve his problem, but can I be
a mirror of the God who, in Jesus, is involved in the
dreams of the people? It is not so much my being able
to do something but my being in solidarity with God's
people. Based on the principle of the incarnation, the

mission of Jesus is to make God known as the God who is involved in human history.

God Reigns over Every Aspect of Life

Many exegetes and theologians agree that if we want to find the central message or the central symbol of the mission of Jesus, it is in the image of the reign of God, the kingdom of God. This kingdom of God declares to the world that now the only ruler will be God, and that all false and pseudo-rulers of the world will be proven false and exposed for what they really are. False and pseudo-rulers are not rulers who will lead people to the real meaning of their lives. It is only when God rules that we will find what it means to live, what it means to be human. We all agree that this reign of God also demands from us a radical decision to choose God—to choose to belong to the reign of God.

If you look at the Gospels, this symbol of the reign of God takes on different forms depending on the type and context of the people being addressed by Jesus. For example, when Jesus encounters a person possessed by demonic powers, he brings the reign of God in a way appropriate to the condition of that person. When Jesus meets with the rich man Zacchaeus, the reign of God is brought in a way suited to this rich man. When he encounters a tax collector like Levi, it is the same kingdom of God but with a bit of difference. When Jesus encounters a widow who has lost her only child, the reign of God comes, but in a way special to this widow. When Jesus encounters a thief on the cross, the kingdom of God is also promised, but in a way that is unique to this thief.

What am I pointing to here? From the perspective of the mission of Jesus focused on the reign of God, we also have the polyvalence and richness of mission; Jesus enables people to proclaim the reign of God in a way suited to each person's experience. The reign of God speaks to all people such that God will be all in all. Therefore, Jesus enables us to hear and to see God in our own experience—to see God in times of plenty, in times of peace, in times of war, in times of economic crisis, in times of personal loss. At every moment of our lives, God can reign. There is no moment in life when the reign of God is not an appropriate message.

Pope Paul VI in *Evangelii nuntiandi* says that evangelization is supposed to bring the good news to all strata of human existence, from human conscience to human structures—economic, political, social, and cultural. The reign of God must penetrate all areas of human life, and at the same time, this reign of God will expose the false gods and rulers that we have allowed to dominate our lives. If we allow God's reign to penetrate all conditions of life, all of our pseudo-rulers, including our pride and our desire for recognition, will be exposed. Hopefully, they will be dethroned, and only God will rule.

There is no human condition that is alien to God. Jesus assumed the human condition in its totality. He knows what it means to be hungry, to be full, to smile, to cry, to dream, to be frustrated, to win some, to lose a lot—he knows all that is human except sin. Because the incarnation brought Jesus to an assumption of all these aspects of human life, the reign of God can be brought there too. There is no human condition that is alien to mission. Part of the mission of Jesus is to reveal a God who can rule in every aspect of life.

God Rules in Insignificance

The mission of Jesus in the incarnation happens in insignificance, in hiddenness, and in seeming failure. This point is not to be dismissed. It is not just by chance that it is part of Jesus's proclamation of who God is.

Jesus in his mission reveals a God different from other rulers—a God who will rule but in a different way. God does not rule by power, by success, by popularity, by a sense of achievement. The mission of Jesus is to be carried out in the spirit of insignificance, in hiddenness, and in seeming failure.

For the church in Asia, mission could be done in the spirit of the incarnation by going back to Jesus and the early church—the church without privileges, the church of martyrs, and the church in catacombs rather than the church of fame, wealth, and power. I also want to think of the church in the Philippines being inspired by the National Mission Congress, saying, "We want to be missionary." But I want to see that church make the decision to be a missionary in Asia in hiddenness, in insignificance, and in poverty. The mission of the Incarnate Word of God took the form of servanthood, a servant who washes the feet of others, proclaiming a God who rules, but who rules as servant. The mission of the Incarnate Word took the form of someone in solidarity with the suffering and persecuted ones.

Our own Asian theologian Felix Wilfred reminds us that mission in Asia can only be effective if it takes the perspectives of the victims and poor whose dreams and hopes will explore for the church the hopes of the Asian peoples for the coming millennium. We are back to *Gaudium et spes*—the hopes and joys, the griefs and anxieties of the men and women of our time, especially of the poor and those who are in any way deprived, these are the same hopes and joys, griefs and anxieties of the followers of Christ.

How can we be missionary? How can we be a mission church following the incarnation if we come in pomp and circumstance? The mission of the Incarnate Word reveals a God who stands by victims, who allows himself to be a victim along with the other victims. The God that Jesus reveals fulfills the God already seen in Exodus, the God who said to Moses, "I have seen the afflictions of my people. I have heard their cries. I know their sufferings." After seeing, hearing, and knowing these things, God made them his very own. All of this is fulfilled in the mission of Jesus.

Now, could the church in the Philippines be missionary in some other way? I do not know. I do not know what type of God we would be revealing if we do not tread the path of insignificance, simplicity, poverty, and even the readiness to become failures. A church that always wants to succeed and prove its achievements—I do not know whether such a church will be in harmony with mission understood within the horizon of the incarnation.

In sum then, the mission of Jesus flowing from the incarnation is making known: (1) a God who gets involved in human history; (2) a God who is able to penetrate and rule every aspect of human life and existence; and (3) a God who rules in insignificance, in hiddenness, in pain, and in poverty.

The Genesis of Christian Mission

I go to the First Letter of John as the paradigm for understanding the origins of Christian mission. We are all familiar with this text where the apostle says and I paraphrase, "What we have seen with our eyes, what we have touched with our hands, what we have heard, about the word of life, we now proclaim to you so that you may have communion with us and our communion is a communion with the Father and with his Son, Jesus Christ."

I think it is a beautiful summary of how Christian mission began. Christian mission began with an experience. It began with someone who had seen, touched, and heard Jesus, the Incarnate One, and who had seen, touched, and heard the Father in Jesus. That experience was a gripping experience of faith, an experience that turned someone into an apostle. Such an experience is the essence of an encounter with the Risen Lord, like the one that transformed a timid Peter into a courageous apostle. It is this gripping experience that transformed Paul the persecutor into the great apostle to the Gentiles.

Christian mission ultimately arises from a gripping experience of the God revealed by Jesus. Not the God that I have read about, nor the God that I have put in a footnote in my grand dissertation. Not the God that I have heard others talk about, but the God that I have seen, touched, and heard—the God revealed by the Incarnate One. This experience can transform me. It can make me an apostle. It can make me a missionary with a very simple code—not to conquer the world, but simply to narrate my story so that those who hear of my experience may be drawn to the same experience.

When you have good news coming from a lived encounter, you do not even need to be told to proclaim it—the very power of the experience impels you to proclaim it. And, like Saint Paul, I will say, "Woe to me if I keep quiet." This is a cardinal rule of every zealous missionary involvement—a gripping experience of the Word of God made flesh. This is good news, so good that I cannot keep it to myself. I have to go around running, walking, even kneeling, just to tell it so that other people may also experience this Word of God. And if two of us have the same experience, that communion is our communion with God in Jesus Christ.

The Figure of the Christian Missionary

Who *is* the Christian missionary? What *is* a Christian missionary church? I think the Christian missionary is someone who has experienced Jesus, the Incarnate One, and whose identity, life, and work are shaped by this experience in faith. Therefore, the missionary becomes through this encounter the embodiment of mission. There comes a point where mission is not simply work to be done; rather, mission and the missionary fuse and become one. This must arise from a gripping experience similar to the one that Jesus, the original missionary, had.

Jesus was possessed by this experience of *Abba*. He was so in love with *Abba*, fascinated by *Abba*, that he could not stop talking about *Abba*. He could not stop telling people, showing people the love of his Father, even as it took him to the cross, to the last moment of his life. There was no stopping him because it came from a transforming experience. If Jesus became a missionary because of such an experience, then how could we not follow the same path? We have Lorenzo Ruiz and Pedro Calungsod—people who were transformed by their experience of Jesus.

A few weeks ago I was in Malaysia. I was invited to be an evangelizer. I had thought that I was the missioner giving lectures for six hours. I thought that it bore some fruit. At the end of the day some participants who graduated from Loyola School of Theology and lay leaders spoke about their difficulties as Christians in Malaysia. One lawyer was imprisoned for helping a Muslim woman who wanted to convert to Christianity. She had to leave Malaysia and was baptized in Australia. Later, she married a Catholic. The Malaysian government went looking for the woman, but it could no longer find her. Instead, it found and imprisoned him. As these participants spoke of mission, this lawyer said, "We should not keep quiet. We should not keep quiet out of fear. No. We should tell people about God and how God liberates in Jesus. I'd go to prison again." He is mission.

Mission is not just work. Jesus, the Incarnate One, is mission. Hopefully, I am mission. Hopefully, we are mission. And hopefully, the church in the Philippines may become mission. We pray for that.

5

Encountering the Asian Face of Christ

In 1993, Orbis Books published a book entitled *Asian Faces of Jesus*, edited by R. S. Sugirthirajah. Not just one Asian face, but Asian *faces* of Jesus. The book also makes the distinction between Jesus and Christ. Why would we even consider something like the Asian face or Asian faces of Jesus Christ? What is in the face? What is the face?

Greek philosophers say that we find in the face a window to the deeper reality that a person possesses. If we want to hide what is really happening within us, many times what we do is change our face. There are faces that are very transparent. You see if they are angry, happy, or if they are by nature good. There are faces

Adapted from a lecture delivered at the Update on Christology Seminar at Loyola School of Theology, Loyola Heights, Quezon City, April 24, 2001.

that cannot hide anything, but there are those who, if they want to hide something, will change their face. That is why some people wear different masks.

The face is really a window into a deeper reality. Some people would even say that the face, to use a more theological term, is one of the most powerful sacraments of who we truly are. The human face is an instrument that conveys something that people do not always see—what we have in our hearts—and, at the same time, veils a deeper reality. We cannot think that everything a person is can be found in his or her face.

What is the face of Christ? Why do we even wonder about the *Asian* face of Jesus?

Jesus, just like any human being, has a unique face. What is the point of talking about the Asian face of Jesus? He has one face. If you are Filipino, then you have a Filipino face. We do not worry about our African face, our South American face, or our Caucasian face. In fact, people will laugh at us, and we will look stupid if we force our Filipino faces to look American by wearing colored contact lenses to have blue or green eyes, or even by dyeing our hair blond while our black eyebrows give us away. For myself, whichever way you look at it, I am Filipino, but I look Chinese. Now, will it make sense for *me* to explore the African face of Jesus or the Caucasian face of Jesus?

How is it that when you are talking about Jesus, this particular Jew, it is quite legitimate to speak of the Asian face of Jesus? For example, in some parishes in North America that are predominantly African American, you will find Jesus depicted as a black person. When you go to China you will find Our Lady depicted as a Chinese woman, and the baby Jesus looking just like *me*. Why is it that we, who are all human beings, find it ridiculous to explore different faces coming from different cultures? We insist, "No. This is my only face." Whereas in the person of Jesus Christ, spiritual writers and theology teachers talk about the different faces of Jesus. What does this say about Jesus?

The Particularity of Jesus and His Universality

Now we shall talk about this dynamic tension between Jesus as a particular person—who lived in a particular place, a particular time, and within a particular culture—and his universal significance. We do not deny the particularity of Jesus. If we deny it, it is tantamount to denying the very humanity of Jesus. For to be human means you belong to a particular family; you belong to a particular race; you belong to a particular generation; and you survive and live in a particular place. To deny this concrete, cultural, and human face of Jesus as a Jew is also to deny that the incarnation is real. It might be that you think of Jesus as an abstract reality. Jesus was truly human, with a particular human face. He was a Jew of the first century, belonging to a particular family and a particular economic class. Jesus had *that* face, that *specific* face.

However, our faith also tells us that Jesus has universal significance, especially in his resurrection. Many theologians will say that, in the resurrection of Jesus from the dead, the human Jesus—this particular Jew—has been universalized in the power of the Spirit so that the risen Jesus is no longer to be equated purely and simply with this particular Jew. The universal Jesus is now able to penetrate different cultures and enter our hearts through the power of the Spirit.

As the Risen Lord made universal by the power of the Spirit, Jesus becomes available to all. Annie can now have a unique experience of Jesus that allows her to say: "My Jesus. My experience of Jesus. This is the face of Jesus that I have encountered." Annie's experience of Jesus may be unique when compared with Marilou's experience of Jesus. They can see the same Jesus, but because of the universal quality of the Risen Lord, Jesus can now be experienced by individuals from different cultures and according to their situations.

For example, what if I had to preside at two funeral masses, one after the other? Let us say the first is for an eight-year-old girl. Yesterday, on a flight back to Manila, I read in a newspaper article that an eight-year-old girl in Bologna, Italy, was murdered by her brother-in-law. When they caught the brother-in-law, he just said, "For a number of days now I've been wanting to have sex with a girl. She was the first person I saw." When asked by investigators why he went to the extent of killing her, he replied: "Because she scratched me. I don't want anyone harming me that way. It irritated me, so I had to kill her." The girl's body was discovered on the eve of her ninth birthday. If I were to preside at her funeral mass, how would I preach about Jesus? What face of Jesus would I manifest to this family? And what if, right after that funeral, I had to preside at the funeral mass for a Chinese trillionaire who died in the intensive care unit of a fabulous hospital? What face of Christ should I show?

It will be the same Jesus Christ but in a different way. It is not only Jesus that must be shown. The different situations of human beings—our needs and conditions—elicit the face of Jesus. Even during Jesus's ministry, he had one message—the reign of God—but that reign of God took on different faces depending on the people Jesus encountered. For the widow of

Nairn, the kingdom of God was shown through the return to life of her child. For Zacchaeus, what was the face of the reign of God? Restitution. "I give half of my belongings to the poor." And so there are different ways; even in the Bible, the message of Christ takes on different faces.

In the resurrection Jesus has become a universal presence. When we say that he is universal Lord and the Savior of all, he is now able through the power of the Spirit to enter human hearts set in different cultures, different families, and different human conditions. As Jesus enters them and assumes them, we find that we discover a different face, a unique face of Jesus.

Before I went to Rome last week, I spoke with two people, one of whom was a woman. I asked how she was, and she replied that she did not have a lot of health problems.

I said, "Oh, we have to thank God because you are not so sick now." (Before, she would complain of such and such illness.)

She said, "But of course I'm not supposed to get sick. I'm a good person. I'm helpful to other people, so it's only just that God reward me."

For her, that was the face of Christ.

The other person I spoke with was a young man whose sister was raped a few years ago.

"How is your sister?" I asked.

He replied, "We seem to have reconciled ourselves a bit to what happened."

I remember this man because he went on retreat after that incident. He was really struggling, and as I talked with him during his retreat he said: "I do not understand why God allowed this to happen. Why was God not able to rescue my sister? Why did he not help my sister?" Some nights he would think about her struggle, her being overpowered, and ask, "God, where were you? Why did you not use your power? Why did you not intervene?"

He continued to pray. He told me, "You know, Father, the Lord showed me something."

He said that it was as if the Lord told him in prayer: "How could I have helped your sister? I was also suffering with her. She was not the only victim. I was a victim with her. And I am a victim like her—torn, unjustly treated. I am one of you." His is a different face of Jesus. It consoled him.

He said: "For me, it is enough that my sister was not alone, that Jesus was being crucified with her. There was someone with my sister." I do not know whether people will like that face of Jesus, or whether you think his conclusion is justified.

Yes, this topic is all about the formal theological question of the particularity of Jesus and his universality. As a particular individual, he had a definite Jewish face. Yet our faith also tells us that he has universal significance. This universal significance allows Jesus to be incarnated in an analogous way—not that the incarnation that happened in the womb of the Virgin Mary will happen again—but the universal savior Jesus Christ is now able to assume different human conditions. And from within those human conditions—different cultures, different human struggles—Jesus is now able to show the power of the same gospel addressing the unique experience of each individual.

This discussion is not merely because it is a fashionable topic. This is about a very, very difficult question: the particularity of the human Jesus and his universal significance. There is a tension. Later, I will indicate a few problems being raised by our brothers and sisters in Asia on this area of the particularity of Jesus and his universal significance.

How Can the Face of Jesus Be Asian?

Religious and Cultural Realities in Asia

An important background to this issue is that in Asia, we have two-thirds of the world's population. It is also in this most populous section of the world where Jesus is the least known and accepted. In fact, half of the Catholic population in the whole of Asia is found in the Philippines. We make up half of the Christians in the whole of Asia. Half of the Christians in Asia are squeezing into this small country of ours, whereas the continent is so large. With our birth rate it might even be that we will have more than half of the Christians. And then you have the Filipinos who go overseas, but they go to the United States, Canada or Europe. They should just go to Bangladesh, Pakistan, Thailand, or Indonesia. I'm asked to give so many lectures here in the Philippines, especially if there are conventions or congresses. It makes me think sometimes, "I'm giving another talk in this place, but these people are already Christians."

This is the problem: Jesus is least known in Asia, the most populous area of the world. There is also the accusation that Jesus is not easily accepted in Asia because he is perceived as Western, a foreigner. Some say that many Asian peoples find Jesus as some sort of an outsider, an intruder who—at least in some sectors of Indian society—will destroy their Indian culture. There are those who say that you have to abandon your being Asian the moment you accept Jesus Christ.

When the Holy Father came to Asia in November 1999, specifically to New Delhi, for the promulgation of the apostolic exhortation *Ecclesia in Asia,* I was asked to attend. It was really a sad occasion. From the airport in New Delhi to the cathedral, I saw only one welcome sign for the Holy Father. It was a big poster saying, "Welcome, Your Holiness, Pope John Paul II." That was it. During those three days some extremists went on national television and in the local papers saying, "Pope, get out of India." "Catholic Church, get out of India." I saw an interview of one leader who said: "We do not want Christianity here in India because Christianity will destroy our Indian culture. Christianity does not respect India. Jesus is like those *conquistadores* from the West who will come here in order to invade and take over."

In *Ecclesia in Asia* we find the Holy Father making a vigorous assertion—Jesus was born on Asian soil. Jesus is Asian. Do you believe that?

The "Asian-ness" of Jesus

Ecclesia in Asia is like a compilation of the fruits of the Synod of Bishops for Asia held in Rome in 1998. During the synod I distinctly remember something that happened as the Holy Father was leading us in prayer to open the session of that day. After the chanting of the psalms, the Holy Father grabbed the microphone, looked into the eyes of the bishops of Asia present in that hall, and said, "Let me remind you, Jesus was born on Asian soil." As he said that, there was complete silence. It was as if nobody could believe—even among the bishops of Asia—that Jesus was really one of us. Afterward, everyone stood up and everyone clapped. It was as if in people's minds they were thinking: "Wow! It is not true that Jesus is Western. Jesus is one of us."

That fact was verified by the attendance of bishops in the Synod of Bishops for Asia. In the thinking of the church, Asia starts in what is called the Middle East and extends to the Far East or to South East Asia. But the Holy Father was also saying that Jesus was born in a part of Asia that was open to the rest of the world—the Mediterranean area. While Jesus is Asian, he cannot be claimed by Asia as though he does not belong to the rest of humanity. Yet, one point that the Holy Father kept on repeating during the synod was, "Remember, Jesus was Asian."

For all the faults of *Ecclesia in Asia,* that is one thing, I think, that people have not explored. How do we rejoice over the fact that Jesus, the incarnation of the Word of God, is Asian? How do we rejoice over God's mysterious plan to send his only Son as a human being and choose a particular people for his incarnation? And that particular people has an Asian heritage? A heritage from the East?

Since 1999 I have been invited three or four times to talk about the Asian qualities of Jesus in the United States and Europe. These Westerners are very excited about it. For two years in a row I have been asked to give a similar workshop, The Asian Qualities of Jesus, in Los Angeles, California. At the end of these workshops people come and congratulate us. "We're very happy. Jesus is one of you!" "What does it mean to be Asian?" "Help us understand the Asian face of Jesus through scriptures."

With the Holy Father, the bishops of Asia have affirmed that we in Asia should recover the "Asian-ness" of Jesus and rejoice that the incarnation happened in Asia. Abraham was Asian. Miriam and Mary were Asians. Joseph was Asian. Aaron and other women and men of the faith were Asians. Jesus himself was Asian.

If we want to discover the Asian face of Jesus, that is, his true face as an Asian, we should go to the scriptures. Let us look at how he taught, how he talked with people, and how he related with them. Look at how he bore suffering. Look at how he dealt with erring people. Look at how he touched. Not only will you see Jesus's face, but you will also see yourselves as Asian. If you calmly and prayerfully try to discover the Asian qualities of Jesus, you will come to discover who you are.

Let me just tickle your imagination. How did Jesus talk about the reign of God? Through the parables—with images of the yeast, fishing, a wedding banquet—which is very Asian. His method of teaching was storytelling. Is it not the case that we Asians like to tell stories? It is difficult to have a teacher who is always talking in abstract concepts. I always tell stories. If you do not understand the stories, then you will not be able to understand the concepts. That is the Asian way. Asians understand stories, and Jesus knew that.

The mind of Jesus is also very relational—the Father and I are one. I do only what I see the Father doing, and I say only what I hear the Father say. For the Western mind it is unacceptable that a thirty-three-year-old does not know what decision to make or is not able to work on his own. We Filipinos try to do the same thing. Young people are already supposed to be independent. Look at Jesus. He is near death, and what does he say? "I do not do anything of my own accord. I do only what I see the Father is doing." There is no dichotomy in Jesus between his submission to the Father and his independence. His autonomy is precisely located in his full submission of self.

At an early age our children are told to be independent. When they grow old, they have a midlife crisis, and we give them a seminar: Healing the Inner Child. Well, maybe we should not hurt them in the first place.

Jesus was perpetually a child. That is Asian. And the Asian parent, no matter what, cannot let go. That is also part of the suffering of God. God suffers the Asian way. The tears of God are the tears of one who cannot let go of children, even if the children are already erring children.

God says in Hosea: "Get out of my sight. Go back, Ephraim. I send you back. I do not care anymore." But after a few verses God says, "How can I give you up, Ephraeim?" Very Asian. "I will never abandon you." Now this is a suffering that saves. Instead of venting my anger to destroy you, my suffering saves you. I suffer, but as I suffer, you are saved.

Jesus, even in the resurrection, continues to be Asian. His students already failed their test during the crucifixion, but when he rose from the dead, he told Mary Magdalene, "Go to my brothers." He still calls them brothers. If I have a student who is failing, I just give him a passing grade. I do not want to see him anymore the following year. But Jesus is really Asian. He was the one who was hurt. He was left behind, and yet he is the one who reaches out to them. Look at his teachings, his manner, his style of debating. Look at his suffering, and you will discover the Asian face of Jesus. You will smile at some point and say, "We are like this."

Of course, Asia is not a monolithic homogenous reality. There is chopstick Asian, curry Asian, chopsuey Asian, and even shawarma Asian. But there is a common thread. The discovery of the Asian face of Jesus will help us with our mission approaches in Asia by leading people back to the basic story of Jesus. It is a beautiful story. And when we are talking with Asian people, if we are faithful in presenting the story of Jesus, they can easily listen. If they cannot feel the "Asianness" of Jesus, it is because we tell the story differently from how it is written in the Bible.

Remember the parable about the workers hired at different hours? People who have been influenced by a strict understanding of justice, that is, give people what they deserve, are the ones scandalized. One time I attended a Bible sharing of mostly elderly women who were all mothers. I asked them, "Is there a problem with this story?" They said, "None." That is because if you are a mother, all your children are equal. It is not because the eldest is thirty years old and another is just twelve years old that you give less to the 12-year-old child. They do not even have to go into speculative thinking or reflection regarding the Asian face of Jesus when they read the scriptures.

What do we understand about the cry of Jesus, "My God, my God, why have you abandoned me?" For us Asians, this sense of abandonment can be the cause of our death. When Jesus saw his friends—with whom he had spent so much time, but who nevertheless abandoned him—what was he supposed to feel? Is it not as if God had left him? One way to understand this is my own experience as a student during the last week of my stay in the United States before coming back home in 1992.

My dentist discovered I had a cyst near my sinuses and warned me that it might affect my brain. It had to be removed, and I had the operation a few days before I left. I was trying to pack my things, and I noticed that the community, made up of American priests and seminarians, was avoiding me. No one was talking with me. I said to myself: "This is too much. I lived with them for five years, and they know that I will be leaving soon. They are not even talking with me. And they know that I had surgery! They are not even commiserating with me."

I was really feeling bad. Then one night the telephone rang in my room. It was one of the seminarians, an American, who whispered, "How are you?"

I said, "Oh, not so good."

He answered, "You know I have been avoiding you."

"Why?"

"Well, you need to rest. You will take this long trip back home, and also you don't need any infections right now. An infection is the last thing that you would want."

So that was what they were thinking.

I told him, "Yes, thank you, but you forget, I am Filipino. We Filipinos don't die of infection. What we *really* die of is isolation! So if you don't want me to die, come down and talk with me."

He had good intentions. But in the hospitals here in the Philippines, isn't it the case that there is an extra bed in the rooms? If you want to kill someone, isolate that person. That was what happened to Jesus. His heart was broken. It was an Asian heart.

During the closing liturgy of the synod in 1998, the Holy Father repeated his reminder that Jesus was born in Asia. Therefore, it is the obligation of Asian Christians to be able to present Jesus in our preaching, in our manner of life, in our church structure, as truly Asian. One proposal is this—can we develop a hermeneutics and biblical exegesis that will be more attuned to the Asian mentality, the Asian way of interpreting texts, in such a way that the "Asian-ness" of Jesus may also shine forth?

One essay in *Asian Faces of Jesus* uses the model of Hindu and Buddhist ways of reading texts. While the historico-critical approach is very good and very precise, I do not know if, for the Asian mind, it is the only way of reading a text. What happens to the figure of Jesus, at least for the Asian, when he is presented to us in this form, as a product of such and such an investigation?

When I was still studying here, I remember my class spending one whole week, four days of one hour each day, talking about the word *dog* in the Gospel where Jesus said, "It is not good to throw the food for the children to the dogs." We spent four hours talking about the word *dog*. What kind of dog was it? Was it small?

Big? Our professor's conclusion was, "Well, in the end, it doesn't change the conclusion of the text." It was a good exercise. But for the Asian mind, is that the way we study and examine things?

From one point of view the Asian face of Jesus is not a matter of speculation. As affirmed by the Asian bishops and the Holy Father, Jesus was born an Asian. Through Jesus, Asian approaches and Asian ways of relating have been incorporated into the word of God and into the gospel. The gospel is not only a written text but also a way of life, a liberating way of life.

Problematic

When we take seriously the Asian face of Jesus, we also get in touch with the reality of Asia. There are many non-Christian faiths in Asia, with some more ancient than Christianity. Since they are more ancient, they are more extensive in their influence. The different cultures of Asia have been shaped by these religions resulting in an intimate union. They really belong together—the cultures constructed by the religions and the religions that are supported by the cultures. Just as it is here in the Philippines. There are those who say that we have a Christian culture because we are predominantly Catholic. The culture supports the church.

Here is the problem. Part of our faith says that this particular human being—Jesus who had a definite face, an Asian Jewish face, is proclaimed by us as the Christ, the Savior. He is not only Savior to a few, but he is the Savior of all. We are making a universal claim for Jesus. He is the Way. He is the Truth. He is the Life. We see this in scriptures. "Nobody comes to the Father except through me." "Jesus is the mediator." The letters of Saint Paul and the Catholic epistles even say: "There is no salvation except through the name of Jesus. There is only one way by which salvation is wrought and it is in the name of Jesus." For us Christians, for us Catholics, this is very normal. The face of Christ, which is very Asian, is also the face of the Savior of all.

However, this poses a particular problem in Asia, because we have so many religions with their own theologies, or, if you want, their own theologies of salvation. These religions all have their own savior figures. The moment we present the Asian face of Jesus, which is at the same time the face of the universal Savior, people from other faiths do not want to accept that face.

In fact, there are many Asian theologians who believe that our exclusive claim of salvation in Jesus destroys the harmony of cultures in Asia. Some propose that we should consider all religions equal so that the face of Jesus is just one of the many possible faces of the incarnation of the mystery of God. They say, "Do not focus so much on the human face of Jesus. Focus on the divine face of the mystery. Be God-centered rather than Jesus-centered." They note that all the other religions focus on God. Our way to God is Jesus Christ. Their way to God is their other savior figures. Then they say, "The Asian face of Jesus. Yes, that's good for you Christians, but do not impose that Asian face of Jesus on all of us as the face of the savior of all."

Then there is a theory of religious pluralism, where all religions are seen as willed by God. It is not just the Judeo-Christian faith that is willed by God, but all religions are willed by God. In other words, all religions are ways to God. So, can the different religions respect one another in the sense of allowing each to prosper? In this theory are we Christians being asked to relativize our absolute claims about Jesus and the church? In the past we Christians held to the teaching that the only true religion is the Catholic religion and that baptism is necessary for salvation. We even had a dictum, which was expressed as "outside the church, there is no salvation."

The Asian face of the unique savior is becoming a problem in Asia. Despite this, we continue to seek the Asian face of Jesus. The Asian face of Jesus can be found in our brothers and sisters in Asia. We do not have to go far to realize that most of those who are suffering and poor in the world are in Asia. In this, the most populous continent of the world, the majority are poor. Therefore, it is mainly in the faces of the suffering victims of Asia, those whom our societies want to bury and forget, that we see the face of Jesus.

In *Ecclesia in Asia* the Holy Father describes Asia not as a geographic space, but as a people with deep thirst and hunger and a yearning for life. The face of Asia, then, is the face of a people searching for life. The Asian face of Jesus is not a topic for speculation. There are some aspects that require serious speculation based on tradition, but in our day-to-day living the Asian face of Jesus may be the face of the next person you meet on the road—hungry, looking for the meaning of life, lonely.

It is like the song that Father Eduardo Hontiveros, SJ, wrote:

> Grant that my eyes
> May truly see
> That you Lord may be found
> In the lowly neighbor
> Jesus my brother

Jesus was born Asian. Today, he is incarnated in this world in myriad Asian ways, especially in the faces of the poor and suffering millions of Asia.

6

Breaking the Isolation
of the Dead

There are many ways of reflecting on the Easter events, especially from Holy Thursday up to the Easter Vigil. This year I was quite fascinated by a framework presented by one of the greatest theologians of our time, Hans Urs von Balthasar. He describes the paschal mystery in terms of movement, movements involving comings and goings. On Holy Thursday Jesus goes to the upper room and to the garden of discernment. On Good Friday he goes to the cross. On Holy Saturday he goes to the dead. On Easter he goes to the Father. In this reflection I concentrate on these last two movements.

On Holy Saturday, or Black Saturday, Jesus goes to the dead. This is part of the Apostles' Creed [ecumenical

---

Adapted from a reflection delivered on Holy Saturday at the Holy Week Triduum at Loyola School of Theology, Loyola Heights, Quezon City, March 30, 2002.

version], but many times we do not notice it or pay much attention to it. We just say that Jesus

> suffered under Pontius Pilate,
> was crucified, died, and was buried;
> he descended to the dead.
> On the third day he rose again.

It is part of the Creed, and yet the power of this belief for our pastoral life and our Christian living—especially for our involvement in the world and in the transformation of society—has not been fully explored. Reflecting on this part of the mystery of Jesus's passion and resurrection can be a powerful force for our conversion and also our apostolic involvement in the world today.

Death as Isolation

First, let me say something about the Jewish worldview regarding death and the place of the dead. After all, the early formulations of the faith were very much influenced by this Jewish worldview. For the Jews, death, like sickness, is an event of isolation. When you get sick, you become isolated. Some are even quarantined. You are given your own room, and nobody is supposed to go into that room.

You are also given your own plate, your own glass, your own spoon and fork, which nobody else should use. Therefore, sickness is the beginning of a slow process of isolation. You cut down on social functions, like not eating with your family, not attending your ballroom dancing lessons, not going to your *mahjong*. There are many things about social life that just collapse with sickness. Someone takes care of you, but no amount of care can remove the fact that with sickness comes a bit of being isolated.

In the Jewish worldview death is the culmination of that isolation. When someone dies, that person, in some sense, is cut off from the world of the living. Where do you go? You go to the place of the dead. The Greeks have a beautiful name for it—Hades. In Hebrew it is Sheol. The dead go to Hades and are called shades. They are like shadows. The shades exist in a form of nonexistence. Why? In Hades, there is no communication among the shades. It may be heavily populated by shades but one thing is missing—communication. The absence of communication is one characteristic of the place of the dead. The dead may be next to one another in Hades, but they do not commune with one another.

Worst of all, in Hades there is no praise of God. People cannot communicate with God. In Hades, that lack of communication with God is real death. Communication with God, especially in the form of adoration or praise, simply stops. Hades is a place where communication with God is not possible. The God of life and the place of the dead simply cannot meet. God, who is Life, cannot have any place in Hades. Therefore, the place of the dead is a place where communion stops—communion among the dead but, worst of all, communion with God.

Death is not just biological. Death is the termination of communication. A person truly dies not only because the biological systems have collapsed. True death is experienced when the possibility of communion, the possibility of personhood, is no longer present. Personhood is actually being in communion with others. If I am not in communion, not able to communicate or to be one with others, then I am dead. More important, when I am no longer able to communicate with God, I am *truly* dead. That is why the dead in Hades do not really exist. They are there physically existing but nonexistent nonetheless because of the absence of the core of life—communion, that is, communication with others and communication with God.

We do not need to die a physical death to be in Hades. Many people are already in the place of the dead because they do not communicate; they are not in communion. You may be in a beautiful mansion and yet live in Hades. When there is no full communion with one another in the same house and full communion with

God, then we are the *living dead*. You can suspect that there are many who are already dead. Simply lonely. Not having anybody to communicate with. Not having someone with whom they can share—not so much their sorrows but, much more difficult, their joys.

I remember one of my most difficult moments as a young priest. I had thought that the most miserable experience was when you were lonely and in pain with no one to share it. That was bad enough, but what was worse was when you were happy and you had no one with whom to share your happiness—then you were really dead. And we are increasing. The number of dead people is increasing.

Some people say that the cell phone is a way of bonding or communicating. Really? Or does it produce more dead people? Once I was invited to bless the house of a family I did not know. The priest who was supposed to bless the house had an emergency, and he gave my name to the family. Since it was an emergency I agreed, but I told them that I had another appointment afterward. I would bless their house and leave immediately for my next appointment. They said, "Good, good. It's okay, Father."

A car came to collect me. The family's three children came along, with one driving the car. No one greeted me. When they learned that I was Father Chito, they just opened the door and I got into the car. From our place to their house, no one was communicating with me. Of course, the driver should not be communicating with me. He had to mind his driving. The two other siblings were not communicating with me because they were busy texting. I said to myself: "Well, it's okay. If they don't want to talk to me then what can I do? I cannot impose myself." But I was already feeling bad.

What somehow calmed me was when I realized that these two siblings were texting one another. They were there in the same car, and they could not even talk with one another. One of them asked the other, "Hey, what is this that you sent? I cannot understand your text. I cannot understand your message."

Instead of explaining it, the other sibling said, "Oh, okay. I will send you another message."

I do not know. Maybe the new name of Hades is "cell phone."

I do not know if we are really bonding in the sense of achieving the fullness of personhood where there are people who can enter my heart and with whom I can also share my heart. In the Jewish worldview that is what life is all about. Life means being in communion with others and with God. When you go to the place of the dead, that communion is cut off. To go to the dead means to go to a place where we experience death in the form of lack of communication, isolation, loneliness, and aloneness.

The Son of God Goes to the Place of the Dead

Jesus did not invent going to the dead. It is part of the Jewish worldview, and as Christians we have retained it. Every person who dies goes to the place of the dead. Given this Jewish background, let our Christian imagination grow and imagine Jesus being buried and going to the dead.

Who goes to the dead? The Son of God. The Son of God goes to the place where God cannot communicate. The Son of God initiates a communication that is impossible and even forbidden by the reality of death. By going to the dead, the Son of God opens a form of communication in a place where communication is not possible. By going to the dead, the Son of God breaks the isolation imposed by death, and he does this freely.

How was he able to go to the place of the dead? By dying himself. The one who goes to the dead is also dead. The One who goes to the place of the dead is one who has also experienced isolation, abandonment, and loneliness. This is why he was able to cry out, "My God, my God, why have you abandoned me?" Quite surprisingly, though he used to call God *Abba,* an endearment of familiarity, he did not use *Abba* on the cross. He went back to the formal address, "My God, my God." There is no familiarity on the cross. There is only abandonment and isolation. He saw his friends watch the crucifixion, but they stood at a distance. The cross was a true death not only in the sense that Jesus breathed his last, but also in the sense that he experienced the loss of communication, the loss of communion. He experienced the agony of isolation. The cross was a real death. When he was alone, it was finished. The death was complete. Now this person who truly died goes to the place of the dead.

Not only is it that the Son of God breaks the isolation of the dead by going to the place of the dead. What is more fascinating is that he was able to go to the place of the dead by being dead himself. He joined the dead in solidarity. What type of solidarity? A solidarity in true death. He did not go to the place of the dead as someone who was strong, as someone who could bring life. No. He went to the place of the dead as someone who also had died, who also had suffered isolation, abandonment, and loneliness. The one who would break the isolation was isolated himself, and only he could break the isolation through solidarity.

Solidarity. By going to the dead Jesus shows the true meaning of solidarity. You go to the dead not with your strength, not with your power, not with what you can give. You go to the dead in solidarity by being dead yourself and, by being dead, you are in deep communion with others. This is the mystery of Holy Saturday. This is the silence of Holy Saturday. Jesus truly dead goes to the place of the dead and breaks the isolation of the dead, but he had to be in isolation himself.

How do we live Black Saturday? A Dutch author said it well: "In our age, we need solidarity, not support." Some people think that when they support a cause or a community, they are already in solidarity with that cause or community. No. The hard teaching of Black Saturday is that solidarity means, with Jesus, I go to the dead to be able to conquer death. But first, I should be with the dead. I should be dead myself, because if I am not dead, how can I go to the place of the dead?

Solidarity means going to a particular community, but not because I am bringing my strength, not because I am bringing my contribution, and not even because I am bringing something it lacks. Solidarity means I go because I am also in need. I bring my needs to their needs. I bring my weaknesses to their weaknesses. I bring my fear and trembling to their fear and trembling. I do not come as someone alive going to the dead. Solidarity means I—the dead—go to the dead.

It seems that support is easier than solidarity. This world does not lack for support because it is easy to do. I send a check and then continue on my own way. By sending a box of instant noodles, I am already able to show my support. My life goes on without significant changes. Black Saturday tells us about the hard lessons of solidarity. We have to remember—the one who goes to the dead is also dead. Only the dead can conquer the isolation of death.

Let me give you a few stories. Sometimes stories better illustrate the mystery. We see that the mystery is truly alive when we look at facts of life and how these mysteries are lived by people.

In 1989, I did some research in Rome and stayed with the Immaculate Heart of Mary fathers. I was the only Filipino in a small community of eight student priests. At that time the superior of the house was a Belgian who had been a missionary here in the Philippines. He had a married cousin who was a bank executive in Rome. During one of his visits with his cousin, he mentioned that there was a Filipino priest living with them. His cousin told him, "Why not invite him to join us for dinner?" And so I was invited.

But I told this Belgian priest, "I don't know your cousins. I might not enjoy the evening." I thought that a meal with strangers would be too uncomfortable, so I declined the invitation.

"But my cousin is insisting because their maid is Filipino and their driver is Filipino."

It was as if I was invited so that they could show that they had a Filipino maid and a Filipino gardener (they were husband and wife). It did not sound good to the ears. I was really offended. But the Belgian priest kept on insisting, and so I agreed to join them for dinner.

True enough, when we arrived at the house, it was the Filipino dressed in a maid's uniform who greeted me at the door. I was introduced to her, and when she found out that I was Filipino too (I look Chinese), she reacted in a typically Filipino way.

"Father! How is the Philippines?" "From where are you in the Philippines?"

I told her I was from Cavite. She and her husband were from the Visayas but grew up in Manila. She was trying to look for some kind of connection between us. You could feel the deep sense of isolation, of losing contact and then, suddenly, there was this chance contact.

She kept asking me about many things, and I answered however I could. I did not even know her, but we continued exchanging stories. At that time I was still living in the United States, and so I really did not know what was happening in the Philippines. It then struck me that I was also isolated. They were isolated, and here I was with them. The ones in isolation met. The dead went to the dead—and there was an explosion of life.

I learned she had a master's degree in education and taught in one of the universities in Manila. Her two children went to medical school, and she and her husband could not support them with just their teachers' salaries. Her husband had taught at the Philippine National Police Academy. She told me, "Father, every day we just forget about our degrees. When we start picking up the laundry or do the dishes, we just try to keep those things from our minds. I don't let it enter my mind that I received a higher education than my employer. I just think of my children." We kept exchanging stories and tears were even shed.

After several minutes the lady of the house came out and said dinner was ready. Her maid was surprised.

"Oh my! I was not able to help out in the kitchen!"

She panicked saying, "Father, just a few minutes. I have to get to the kitchen."

But the Belgian lady stopped her and told her to change her clothes. "No, tonight you will be my guests. Go to your room and get dressed."

The Filipino couple protested.

I spoke to them in Filipino and said, "Go ahead. Give in to their request. Change your clothes."

They went to their rooms and came out wearing beautiful clothes that had obviously not been used for a long time. The woman wore makeup, and her husband wore a *polo barong.* You could see the creases from the folds. They also looked as if they felt awkward in their clothing.

What a dinner it was! The maid sat at one end of the table while the driver sat on the other end. Three of us priests sat with them, and the Belgian couple did not eat. Instead, they served us dinner. I could not eat for sheer joy. Do not ask me what was served; I do not even remember. There was a real sense of liberation. The king and queen of the house became the maid and gardener. They joined the ranks of the dead and started serving. You forgot who was who at that dinner—who the lord of the house was, who the maid was, who the priest was—because it was just one community of life and love. I am sure it was back to normal the following day. Their roles would still be the same. The lord of the house would still be the lord of the house. The maid would still be the maid. However, I am sure that new life has entered that family, a bit of difference, a bit of liberation. That is Black Saturday. People willing to die and in their death—not in their strength, not in their being the giver, but in their nothingness too—life emerges.

I have another story. This happened in one of those counseling situations we priests find ourselves in. When I was a much younger priest, even after all the lessons in school, my concept of counseling was that the counselee was someone in grave need. *Kaya nga pumupunta iyan eh.* [That is why they go to you in the first place.] This person is a bundle of needs, wants, and crises and he chooses to come to me. In other words, he needs something, and I am the one to give him what he needs. He is confused, while I am the picture of lucidity and clarity. Hopefully, after our encounter he will leave with a lucid mind, and I will be left problematic. But that was not what we learned in school.

I was an eager young counselor and spiritual director. I was so eager that when someone came, one look and I knew what the problem was. It was also as if I had a reservoir of solutions. Given such and such a situation, I would give such and such an answer.

Perhaps the counselee said, "Father, I grew up with my grandmother."

Aha! He grew up with his grandmother! He has anger toward his parents. "You have anger," I said. Even if he has yet to tell me his story, I already know what happened. Then you try to convince him that he is angry. He denies it.

"You know you have anger."

"No, Father. I do not feel anything like that."

"You see, you are beginning to raise your voice! Your anger is showing. I am projecting to you the father figure and you, you were not able to release your anger toward your real father. You are doing it to me now."

Ganyan lang tayo eh, lagi tayong magaling. [That is how we are, always the clever ones.] We are not only *magaling* [clever], but we are also omniscient. For every human situation we have an arid analysis, a ready answer. The answer is usually a solution to a problem. I am very, very thankful to one seminarian who had

the courage to tell me in the middle of one spiritual
direction session, "Father, there is something I have to
say to you. You know, you talk too much. I haven't even
told you my story, and yet you already think you know.
You're clever, but what I need is empathy." I stopped at
that point and started reflecting.

What is empathy? Empathy is Black Saturday. You
encounter people, especially in their neediness, in their
darkness, in their worst confusion. As you encounter
them, encounter them as dead yourself. Do not pretend
that you are the stronger one or the wiser one. *Hindi
totoong kulang-kulang sila at ikaw buo.* [It is not true that
they are incomplete and you are whole.] For me, that
was a wonderful lesson.

I was also taught another lesson in a counseling situation. As this person told me the story of his life, I was
amazed at how he had managed to survive. How could
a person with all those experiences still be here? He
told me about the tremendous dying that he had un-
dergone, and all I could do was just sit there and listen.
I could not really do anything but simply cry with the
person, to be at a loss and admit that I did not know
what to say. As I listened, I also recalled the darkness
and shadows in my own life. I began to wonder whether
I was listening to his story or to mine. In the end, you
think to yourself: "I understand. I know how it feels to

die. I know how it feels to be confused. I know how it feels to be in darkness."

When you have no more words and what you bring is your own helplessness before someone who is equally helpless, problems disappear and the mystery takes over. The person before you is no longer a problem to be solved. That person becomes a mystery that you behold, and you are able to enter into their mystery by accepting your own mystery. In the meeting of these two mysteries, new life erupts. Problems may remain but you now know that you are not alone. You have a friend. You have a companion. You have someone you can empathize with—his tears are your tears, his cries your cries. His gasping breath is your own. Empathy. Solidarity. Black Saturday.

Another story is related to Christmas. I was still a student in Washington, DC, when a Filipino woman friend decided to go home for Christmas after having stayed in the United States for fifteen years. She was so excited that she wrote to a lot of friends and relatives about her vacation. Her friends and relatives were also excited about her visit, especially since it was Christmastime. They wrote her back but, in their letters, they always cautioned her about the law-and-order situation in Manila. She ended up calling me and telling me she was having second thoughts about going home. I told her to go home, but also to be careful and not flaunt her dollars.

She went to Manila for Christmas, but her fear took over. Anywhere she went, she clutched her purse tightly to her chest in fear someone might try to grab it. In her head she was thinking, "These children, these poor people on the streets, they're only out for one thing, out there to abuse. They're out there to steal. I'm the one who just came from the States. I'm the rich person they'll want to steal from." She had a worldview that neatly split the place of the dead—the dirty, the poor, those in need—from her own, which she had to protect.

Just a few days before Christmas she and her brother were driving along one of Manila's main thoroughfares when their car broke down. Her brother, who was driving, said: "I will call a mechanic. Do you want to stay inside the car? We can lock it. Or you can stay outside. We can lock it so if anything happens you can just make a run for it."

She said, "Okay, I'll stay outside." Standing next to the car, she kept praying, "Lord, protect me from hold-uppers. Lord, protect me from beggars. Lord, protect me from *this*. Lord, protect me from *that*." Everything she was afraid of, she asked the Lord for protection. "Lord, protect me. Don't send any children to me. Don't send any beggars to me."

But God sent a beggar, a little boy.

"Miss, we haven't had lunch yet. My mother said that you might be able to help us. Can you give us some money to buy food?" said the boy.

She panicked, opened her purse, and without looking, gave him the first bill she got hold of—which was a large bill. When she saw it, she thought, *"Naku!"* [Oh my]. But she gave it anyway. She gave it not out of charity but with this in mind: "I've given you something. Now leave me alone. Don't bother me anymore. I'm just minding my own business."

Thinking about all those pesos, she worried: "That boy might tell other people that there's a woman giving away pesos in the street. There might be more people who will come asking me for money." All kinds of thoughts were entering her mind. The boy might return and tell her that they do not have food for dinner. She could not stop thinking about it.

The boy did return. He said, "Miss, my mother said the money you gave was too much. There is so much food. You might want to eat with us. Please join us for lunch at our house."

She answered, "I can't go with you. I am watching over the car."

"But we live right there," the boy said, pointing to a shack near the road. The shacks along Roxas Boulevard had plastic shopping bags for walls. "While we're eating, we can see your car."

Something must have happened to my friend, because she followed the boy. She went to the place of the dead.

She went to the shanty and saw the boy's mother, an infant, and three other small children. The first words of the mother to her were, "Miss, the money you gave was too much. Here is the change. I did not know how to get food for my children. My husband hasn't gotten his salary yet. I am so embarrassed, but I cannot do anything else."

My friend then told her: "Go ahead. Keep the money. You might be able to use it for tonight or for tomorrow or for Christmas."

The mother invited my friend to eat with them, and she joined them. She ate with them. She carried the baby and played with the children. She told me that she forgot all about the car. She was just energized by this setting. She also told me that it was the best Christmas dinner she had during that vacation. It was the first time she had ever entered a shanty or held the hand of a poor woman. "That was the first time I was able to carry an infant born to a squatter's family," she said. Then she added, "They're wonderful people."

She went to the place of the dead, but she had to be willfully dead—dead to all of her pretensions and emotions—and only then, by a stroke of grace, when she forgot all about the car and what that car stood for, was she ready to enter the place of the dead. New life sprang forth. It was the best Christmas for her, the best meal. And I'm sure, for that family, it was also a kind of visitation, an experience of grace.

That is Black Saturday. That is solidarity.

Let us join Jesus, the one who embraced death. Let us join him as he goes to the place of the dead and open our eyes to the many manifestations of Hades in our times. Let us hear Jesus calling not only for support but for real solidarity, real empathy, real dying. For only those who have died can break the isolation of the dead.

I would like to conclude these reflections with a prayer:

Heavenly Father, we do not only thank you for the gift of Jesus, but we also want to express to you our puzzlement. This man, your Son who is the giver of life, dies because of our sinfulness and rebellion. Yet we also see that his dying was his solidarity with all who have died—a solidarity that conquers death and its isolation. Thank you for this holy death. Thank you for his descent to the dead.

Help us to die ourselves and give us the humility and courage to go to the place of the dead, not bearing our own strength but bearing our own dying and weakness. For it is only in such solidarity that we create communities, families, neighborhoods and a whole nation of true communion and life.

We beg the Blessed Mother, the woman who died so many deaths, who joined Jesus in his going to the dead through her own pains and sorrows, to always accompany us as we carry our own crosses, as we are crucified, as we die.

Bless those who feel deep loneliness and isolation, those who are poor and victimized because of ignorance, discrimination, and the violence that is in the world. Assure them that the Crucified One has visited them, that they are not alone in the place of the dead. Amen.

7

The Church's Mission
toward Minorities

Theological reflection on the mission of the church toward minorities is the aim of this presentation; I choose a more "theoretical" in comparison to an "existential" approach. While it is true that no serious reflection is done apart from people's life experiences and situations, it is equally true that no experience occurs divorced from a horizon of understanding and interpretation. My first goal in this article is to serve theological reflection by articulating a framework within which the church's mission toward minorities can be more adequately understood. A second goal is to help direct, or redirect, the actual performance of mission toward minorities.

Adapted from an article originally published as "Der Auftrag der Kirche gegenüber Minderheiten," in *Zeichen unter den Völkern: Die prophetische Kraft christlicher Minderheiten* (Munich: Missio, 1996): 83–86. Also published in *Landas* 14 (2000): 129–39.

In the first part of the article, the situation of being minority or belonging to the minority is dwelt upon. The second part shows how the church's appropriation of the situation of the minority can reinterpret the understanding of its mission. The type of church that emerges from mission recast according to the optic of the minority is considered.

It will be obvious, as the argumentation of the article unfolds, that mission will not be interpreted exclusively as work or task performed for minorities. Rather, it will be approached as a moment of mutuality between the church and the world of the minorities. Consequently, mission will be considered as generative of the *ekklesia,* of the church's being, identity and rebirthing rather than simply a pragmatic "spelling out" of an a priori ecclesial essence.

Describing the Minority Reality

We begin by reflecting on the situations of people who are part of a minority. Talk about minorities usually focuses on people who, as a group, are numerically fewer than other groups who make up the wider society. This quantitative notion of the minority status is easily verifiable in the case of migrants and foreigners, of cultural, religious, and ethnic groups who form small pools or pockets within a much larger population. It is in this numerical sense that Christians are considered a minority in most countries in Asia. This signification also lies behind the observation that, within the church, the Caucasians—who were 80 percent of the whole Christian population in 1900—will be a minority by the year 2020, when they will make up a mere 20 percent of the total number.[1] On this level of understanding, to belong to the minority means "to be one of the few" living in the midst of "others" who en masse constitute "the more, the majority" of society. The statistical approach to the minority situation, however, does not capture the full reality of belonging to the minority.

When the discussion moves to the level of quality of life, the minority condition acquires a new configuration. The focus shifts from numbers to *actual people* who experience being regarded as lesser in rank or importance within a societal hierarchy. In some cases it comes in the form of being considered as not having come of age or as not possessing the normative "maturity" supposedly already achieved by other sectors of society.

This qualitative dimension of the minority situation deserves greater attention because of the neglected

---

[1] Robert Schreiter, "The Theological Meaning of a Truly Catholic Church," *New Theology Review* 7 (1994): 7.

and, therefore, powerful truth it forces upon our consciousness. The numerical minority does not automatically become the qualitatively "least" in a given society, as evidenced in the cultural superiority of a small elite. Conversely, the statistical majority may, in fact, be living in a minority state of existence. When the church is called to conversion to the cause of minorities, it is primarily in the qualitative sense that the word *minorities* is taken. Let us turn to three examples of people whose living experiences illustrate minority situations.

The first big group of minorities, who incidentally make up the larger part of humanity, is the so-called Third World, the reality of which exists even within countries of the so-called First World. These are people who suffer subjugation at the hands of holders of power. Deprived of real opportunities to attain a decent human life, and often of their cultures and identities, they are subjected to different forms of crucifixion, meriting for them the name "crucified peoples," victims who remind us of the presence of executioners.[2] From the eyes of the Third World, belonging to the minority is perceived as poverty imposed on the weak by dominant powers.

A second group is composed of the migrants. Now present globally, they are living narratives of life as

---

[2] Jon Sobrino, "The Crucified Peoples: Yahweh's Suffering Servant Today," in *1492–1992: The Voices of the Victims,* Concilium 1990/6, ed. Leonardo Boff and Virgil Elizondo (London: SCM Press, 1990), 120–21.

minority. Whether refugees, skilled or unskilled laborers, they remind the world of ethnic conflicts, political persecutions, religious or tribal wars, famine and imbalances in international political, economic and cultural relations that have forced them into geographical and cultural displacement.[3]

The presence of migrants often generates xenophobic and discriminatory reactions from the dominant racial or cultural group, thereby making the migrants the easy scapegoat of national ills and restrictive laws. Though they contribute also to the economic and social life of the receiving countries, the positive side of their cultures is not appreciated. Defensiveness and self-centered restrictions are the responses they usually get.[4] Effectively excluded from what is significant in society, they are debased mainly on the basis of their ethnic background or race, which is judged to be inferior to that of the dominant sector.[5]

Finally, there are women. According to feminist scholars, the minority status of women is due to sexism, a pattern of attitudes and structures analogous to

---

[3] Silvano Tomasi, "The World-wide Context of Migration: The Example of Asia," in *Migrants and Refugees,* Concilium 1993/4, ed. Dietmar Mieth and Lisa Cahill (London: SCM Press, 1993), 3–4.

[4] Ibid.

[5] Paul Schotsmans, "Ethnocentricity and Racism: Does Christianity Have a Share in the Responsibility?" in Mieth and Cahill, *Migrants and Refugees,* 87–89.

ethnocentrism and racism. Sexism considers women as essentially inferior to men and flawed in humanity on the basis of physical and psychological traits. Women stand on the margins of society, being part of the whole yet outside the main body. "Being there [on the margins] signifies being less, being overlooked, not having as much importance."[6]

The faces of the less in rank or importance that we have presented are just a few of the many that could be encountered. But they give us sufficient insight into the world of the minorities, a world generated by the "lack of ease" in dealing with "others" or with "otherness." The experiences of minorities indicate that, very often, difference is understood in terms of exclusive definition or mutual exclusion. In this sense a person or group acquires a unique identity by defining oneself or itself over and against "others." Otherness is not a function of relatedness but of segregation.

This isolationist perspective, when influential in viewing "others," often operates on both cognitive and emotional levels, shaping not only ideas but charging them with strong affective reactions.[7] Because "others" in fact show us who "we" really are, we tend to ignore, cover up, or distort "others" in order to eliminate the

---

[6] Elizabeth Johnson, *She Who Is: The Mystery of God in Feminist Theological Discourse* (New York: Crossroad, 1992), 22.

[7] Schotsmans, "Ethnocentricity and Racism," 91.

threat that they pose to our identity.[8] To appreciate ourselves, we engage in depreciating "others." To preserve society harmony, the plurality that "others" bring is not tolerated. Uniformity is imposed by the logic of domination, not recognition, by the logic of assimilation, not respect.[9]

If the church is to serve minorities, it needs to enter the world created by this lack of ease with otherness. From the Spirit of communion and the Word of love it hears the question, "For you, Church, do they also count as 'others'?" The mission of the church takes shape in the very event by which it helps create a world and a church where otherness is not the stumbling block that it is made to appear.

The Church in Relation to Minorities

The story of Babel tells of how otherness, symbolized by different languages, led to confusion, scattering, and abandonment of the city being constructed (Gen 11:1–9). Babel speaks of otherness as a curse. The day of Pentecost reversed Babel. Mysteriously, the Spirit did not eliminate the diversity of languages but enabled

[8] Sobrino, "The Crucified Peoples," 120.

[9] Johann Baptist Metz, "With the Eyes of a European Theologian," in Boff and Elizondo, *1492–1992: The Voices of the Victims*, 116.

people to understand one another, to gather and to construct a new community (Acts 2:5–12). Pentecost assumes otherness as a blessing in the unifying power of the Holy Spirit. The church's mission toward minorities takes on the Pentecostal thrust of overturning Babel.

Within this general perspective we can identify some priorities that must characterize the church's mission to minorities.

Solidarity-Communion

One mark of the church's service to minorities is facilitating the creation of a new hermeneutical culture both within and without the church, where the recognition of others in their otherness happens within the horizon of a covenant relationship.[10] This entails breaking the prevailing hermeneutic of defining ourselves by withdrawing from "others" or, in the words of Metz, defining "ourselves exclusively with our backs to such faces."[11] Among the manifestations of this prevailing hermeneutic are the tendencies toward mental isolationism, tactical provincialism, existential distance, privatization of lives and the voyeuristic approach of onlookers—all contributory to the suffering of many

[10] Ibid., 117.
[11] Ibid., 114.

in the world. A covenant resting on common humanity needs to be forged again with renewed vigor.

For this to happen, the church must spearhead the movement toward constructive tolerance,[12] not a grudging accommodation of differences but a calm and joyful recognition and integration of other systems of meanings and cultures, allowing them to build up the whole. Inter-culturality therefore becomes an indispensable element of the church's life and mission. Even outside the explicit question of serving minorities, the church needs to grow in this area, especially concerning the concrete communion of local churches within the universal church. The church after Vatican II continues to search for adequate theological and structural responses to the demands of the concrete catholicity of the one church—the one church that exists in and out of local churches *(Lumen gentium,* no. 23).

Respect for human dignity is central to solidarity. In the world of minorities the church has a privileged opportunity to witness to the gratuitous love of God that looks to humans as they are and not to lovable qualities they have to offer or from which one could profit.

This *agape* is the soul of mission.[13] The power of this love impels the church to be of universal service

---

[12] Schotsmans, "Ethnocentricity and Racism," 93.

[13] Yves Congar, "Dieu, qui envoie en mission," *La vie spirituelle* 148 (1994): 494–95.

to people as people, to exist for people even outside its fold, to be universal sacrament for the world.[14] The mission of solidarity requires an "empathetic mysticism of opened eyes,"[15] which sees a neighbor in the "other," in a wounded "foreigner," in the "Samaritan" (Luke 10:25–37).

Solidarity with minorities becomes solidarity with all peoples, especially the suffering and victims. Solidarity, however, becomes truly dynamic and militant only in the practice of radical charity that breaks down barriers that stand in the way of peace.[16] It is commonplace to think of serving minorities in terms of kind acts that are necessary and laudable. But if the world of the minorities becomes an interpretative key to understanding mission, we cannot allow the church to treat the minorities simply as beneficiaries of the church's benevolence. Neither is it sufficient for the church to respond to their needs occasionally, or only in times of emergency. "Solidarity instead of support" is necessary.[17]

---

[14] Ottmar Fuchs, "Church for Others," in *Diakonia: Church for Others*, Concilium 198, ed. Norbert Greinacher and Norbert Mette (Edinburgh: T&T Clark, 1988), 47.

[15] Metz, "With the Eyes of a European Theologian," 119.

[16] Frei Betta, "The Prophetic Diakonia: The Church's Contribution to Forming Humanity's Future," in Greinacher and Mette, *Diakonia,* 57.

[17] Hermann Steinkamp, "Diakonia in the Church of the Rich and the Church of the Poor: A Comparative Study in Empirical Ecclesiology," in Greinacher and Mette, *Diakonia,* 70.

In the face of minorities the church cannot fall back on the inadequate responses of institutionalized *diakonia*—performed by social action centers and diocesan offices—that somehow absolve Christians from effective *koinonia* with the real men and women who inhabit the minority world.[18] Solidarity implies the conversion of the world and of the church to partnership with the minorities who are clamoring for change in the world order. The church, therefore, is critically questioned by the minorities themselves regarding its role in the perpetuation of barriers, of ethnocentrism, of the curse of Babel.[19] Solidarity demands of the church vulnerability and sensitivity to the transforming influence of the world of the minorities.

Mutuality-Complementarity

True communion or solidarity, resting on the foundation of respect for our common human dignity, presupposes a sense of equality among peoples. Christians are a people of the conviction that in Christ all are one—Jew or Greek, slave or free, male or female (Gal 3:28). Equality in turn is manifested in the attitude of mutuality or reciprocity that allows and celebrates

---

[18] Ibid.; cf. Fuchs, "Church for Others," 45.

[19] Walter Lesch, "Nationalism and the Oppression of Minorities," in Mieth and Cahill, *Migrants and Refugees*, 118–19.

interdependence and exchange. The power of Pentecost propels the church's mission and creates a world of mutuality within the church—a church of diverse elements that complete each other and make the body whole (1 Cor 12).

While solidarity affirms the blessing in otherness, mutuality affirms as strongly that we are and become what we are, not in spite of, but because of "others." Otherness is rooted in a deeper communion of equals from whom differences or manifestations of otherness spring. This communion is not lessened or threatened by otherness, because it is precisely otherness that makes the whole what it is. Otherness is assumed within a more fundamental unity by making that unity depend on the mutuality of those who are "other." Mission toward minorities attempts to make mutuality a pillar on which human relationships in the world and in the church should stand.

If mission is set within the perspective of promoting mutuality and complementarity, then the church will become a community where "helpers" and those "helped" assume both roles. The church will be the first to learn that the suffering people do not only have a claim to the help of "others," but also "they always have something important to say as well."[20] Mission is

---

[20] Fuchs, "Church for Others," 46.

concretely experienced in the birth of a "complementary community" described by Fuchs as mutual fellowship of helpers and those who need help, the healthy and the sick, the strong and the weak, where roles can be exchanged. "Others" are not looked upon in a patronizing manner but appreciated in their potential for enriching others as they are. Talking of this complementarity, the Second Plenary Council of the Philippines said, "In the Church, nobody is so poor as to have nothing to give, and nobody is so rich as to have nothing to receive."[21]

When we consider the minorities in terms of their victimhood, mutuality demands that their salvific role in the history of the world and the church be recognized. As we bring the crucified peoples down from their crosses, we receive from them the salvation that they so eloquently bring to humanity: hope, great love, forgiveness, solidarity, and faith.[22] The minorities have an evangelizing and humanizing potential in their offer of community, cooperation, simplicity, and openness. They shed a light that unmasks the lies and pretensions of societies. Often the minorities evangelize through the disquieting yet salutary questions they put to the "helpers" who must recognize their own poverty and need for help. "The person who suffers always has an

---

[21] *Second Plenary Council of the Philippines: Acts and Decrees* (Manila: Catholic Bishops' Conference of the Philippines, 1992), no. 98.

[22] Sobrino, "The Crucified Peoples," 125–26.

essentially critical, transforming and intensifying quality for all concerned."[23]

Again, the Second Plenary Council of the Philippines states that the "Church of the Poor" is not only a church that evangelizes the poor but where

> the poor will themselves become the evangelizers. Pastors and leaders will learn to be with, work with, and learn from the poor. A "church of the poor" will not only render preferential service to the poor but will practice preferential reliance on the poor in the work of evangelization.[24]

Thus a vision of a renewed community—where everyone has an indispensable and active role in the building up of the whole—is opened up. The minorities are no longer regarded as less in rank, importance, maturity, or culture. They possess the dignity of evangelizers and helpers.

Prophetic Witness to Eschatological Hope

Very briefly, we have to articulate how mission, understood as solidarity and mutuality, becomes the

---

[23] Fuchs, "Church for Others," 46.

[24] *Second Plenary Council of the Philippines: Acts and Decrees*, no. 132.

very prophetic witness to eschatological hope that the church is meant to offer. Certainly the "church is not primarily a moral institution, but the bearer of a hope. And its theology is not primarily an ethic but an eschatology."[25] The hope that Christians bear is not a false optimism that denies the cries of sorrow and mourning arising from the bowels of history and the earth. Hope, rather, assumes the ambiguities of human situations, the pains of victims, the degradation of "others," and from within them continues to believe in a future firmly held out to us. Hope asserts that the dehumanization of "others" does not have the last word; rather, the reconciled and redeemed humanity born on the cross of Jesus has won and will triumph.

This mission of hope is the only way for the church to witness to the Christian God, the God of life. Other gods are kept alive by the sacrifice of human lives, especially of the poor. By struggling for a form of solidarity that respects mutuality, the church not only struggles for the liberation of minorities but at the same moment gives witness to the God of life and the God of love.[26]

---

[25] Metz, "With the Eyes of a European Theologian," 116.

[26] Betta, "The Prophetic Diakonia," 61; Congar, "Dieu, qui envoie en mission," 491–92.

Conclusion

Whether the church in a particular human setting occupies a qualitatively majority or minority position becomes rather immaterial in the perspective of mission we have taken. Whether the church is influential or not in its given human space, the calling to opt for the least, for the marginalized "others," is constant. By taking on the world created by alienating otherness, the church renews its mission and itself in a vision of blessed otherness. Solidarity and communion, mutuality and complementarity, and hope become the foci of its mission and its identity. In the performance of mission, the church becomes, cannot help but become, the community where "others" will find a home, a truly catholic church, a credible universal sacrament of salvation, a prophetic bearer of hope. Then the church truly becomes an icon of the one God it believes in: one God in three different Persons, whose otherness springs from their relatedness and communion of life and mission.

8

A New Person
with a New Mission

We join Jesus in the event of Easter and tonight we shall already celebrate that passage from the darkness of death to the dawn and the light of the risen Christ. Of course, the whole paschal mystery cannot be chopped up as though the different segments can stand by themselves without relying on how we think in terms of time and space. We need to think of a Holy Thursday. We need to think of a Good Friday. We need to think of a Black Saturday. But we have to remind ourselves that this is one total mystery. I cannot say, "My favorite is Good Friday. I don't care about Holy Thursday, Black Saturday, and Easter Sunday." Others say, "My favorite is Easter. Just let me pass Good Friday and Black Saturday."

Adapted from a reflection delivered on Holy Saturday at the Holy Week Triduum at Loyola School of Theology, Loyola Heights, Quezon City, March 30, 2002.

We cannot choose one and neglect the others. It must be a total approach to the one mystery.

But since we are conditioned by time and space, we have to dwell on the different dimensions and locate them in terms of a timeframe. However, as different Bible scholars and theologians try to recover this sense of mystery, sometimes the consideration of time and space disappears. This is a reminder that the descent to the dead already brings with it the promise of resurrection. The way we tell these stories seems as if Easter and the descent to the dead actually coincide. It is one mystery. As you go to the dead, new life is already erupting.

Let us now devote ourselves to the reconsideration of Easter. Borrowing from Hans Urs von Balthasar, Black Saturday is going to the dead, and Easter is going to the Father, or maybe even a return to the Father.

Strictly speaking, even if we look at the accounts of the resurrection in the Bible, there are no witnesses to the resurrection. We do not have anyone who can tell us how the resurrection of Jesus happened. What we have are accounts of people who have already experienced the Risen Lord, to whom the Risen Lord has already appeared. They are people who had encountered the Risen Lord, or better, those who had been graced with an encounter with the Risen Lord. But still, there are things that we have to be clear about.

It is now generally accepted, and I think it is a good reminder, that the resurrection is not resuscitation. The resurrection is not simply the return to life of a corpse. Some think of the resurrection as that—what was dead before is now breathing again. If that were the case, then Jesus cannot claim this unique experience of resurrection. It happened to someone already— Lazarus. But we do not say Lazarus was resurrected. Did Lazarus die again? I hope so. If not, where is he? He should be very old by now. But definitely, he died again. In fact, according to the account of the Gospel of John, when many people started believing in Jesus on account of Lazarus, the chief priests, Pharisees, and scribes thought of killing Lazarus. We do not know; maybe they had him killed. But definitely, Lazarus died again. The daughter of Jairus was brought back to life. Jesus said: "Why are you wailing and crying? Why all this noise and din? The girl is asleep." I also think that the girl became an adult woman and eventually died.

But we are proclaiming something else. It is not just resuscitation but resurrection. Resuscitation is a return to life. What kind of life? It is a return to the earthly, historical life. It is life as usual. Business as usual. The drudgery of life. All the crises of life. You return to all of that. You are resuscitated. When I give talks, I ask the people in the audience if they want to go to the kingdom of God. Many people raise their hands. But no hands are raised when I ask, "How many of you want to enter the kingdom of God tonight?" Deep down, what we want is resuscitation, not resurrection. We do not want to leave this world. The faith of Christians proclaims that Jesus is risen. The way it is proclaimed by Saint Paul and other writers leads us to a deeper faith in the resurrection.

We can agree with von Balthasar that one way of looking at the resurrection is that Jesus—the One who was sent by God, came from the Father, humbled himself and fulfilled his mission—returns to the Father when his mission is completed. Now, Jesus lives in the full presence of the Father. His is not just a return to earthly life but an assumption of a new life in the presence of the Father, which is the fullness of life. In the return to the Father, the human life of Jesus and everything that went with it are neither negated nor eliminated. Everything that Jesus said and did was taken by the Father, accepted by him, confirmed, made part of the eternal now, and will not die anymore. It will not pass away. It will not be touched by sin or conquered by death. It will be forever. This life is the acceptable life.

One author even says that when Jesus returned to the bosom of the Father, the Father must have shouted again, "This is my beloved Son!" On the cross, Jesus said: "My God, why have you abandoned me? Where are you?" In the resurrection what he was waiting for was proclaimed. "You are my son. I am well pleased with you. Your life will be eternally present. It will not end anymore. It will not be touched by sin." It is permanent because it is now a human life that has been glorified, accepted by God, and now belongs to the realm of God, to the inner life of God.

This event of the resurrection happened in history, but at the time, because we talk about eternity, it is meta-historical. It is beyond history. The Letter to the Hebrews says that the sacrifice of Jesus on the cross was completed in the heavenly sanctuary. We are crossing the boundaries between earth and heaven, between time and eternity. If you find me struggling for words, it is because this is such a difficult subject. For how can we talk about eternal things with our limited minds and our limited senses? How can we capture eternity? That is why the resurrection, how Jesus actually rose from the dead, is an object of silence in the Bible. And we are happy there is silence to indicate that what was happening was probably beyond what can be written by a human being. Maybe it is even beyond what human beings can think about and see. As you will see during the celebration of the Easter Vigil, and even tomorrow, the resurrection will be celebrated with a lot of symbols. That is what we can afford to use to depict the resurrection—symbols.

There will be darkness and light. The vigil will start with darkness and then the new fire will be lit. Let the symbolism speak. We will be using water—symbols of life and cleansing. We will have many stories—readings from the creation to the liberation of the people of Israel to Abraham and so on until we reach Jesus. The whole symbolism of history and what God is doing in history. There will be plenty of songs tonight. And, of course, the greatest song—the *Exultet*. I have been singing the *Exultet* for twenty years as a priest and have yet to memorize it. I keep forgetting the tune, and I always choke with tears when singing it—you come to that proclamation recalling all the past events leading to this resurrection; you recall how this person is humiliated and insulted; and you even praise God for the sin of Adam, "O happy fault." When you sing this and you feel the tension, how do you sing it? What is the mood? Are you happy? Are you sad? This is all part of the symbolism, and your mind just cannot retain everything.

Easter is eternal. It does not get old. Every year we sing it. We just have to do it in song. Some even dance. Tomorrow we have this *encuentro* (encounter) where the black veil of the Virgin will be removed by a child, who will be very nervous and afraid as he or she plays out this role. Easter is full of symbols. One single symbol is not enough. We keep multiplying the symbols every year, but even with the multiplication of symbols we are still poor. We cannot fully capture the mystery of Jesus's resurrection. The multiplication of symbols simply alerts us to the fact that we are getting poorer and poorer every year. How do we really embrace the mystery of resurrection?

More important for our purposes is for us to realize that the resurrection is meta-historical, beyond history. We are entering eternity. However, we also realize from scripture that this event created new histories in the lives of peoples. It was not only Jesus who rose from the dead and entered the eternal realm of the Father. Because of the resurrection of Jesus, new life and new histories are being experienced by people. It is true that the resurrection was uniquely experienced by Jesus, but it is not contained by Jesus alone. The resurrection is a mystery that is at the heart of our lives too, especially the lives of the baptized.

Let us look at how the resurrection of Jesus Christ has created new histories in the lives of people so that we will be confirmed in our faith that the resurrection is real—Jesus is truly risen. In the end, it is not just words that will proclaim the resurrection of Jesus, but the power of this risen life of Christ to generate new histories. This is the type of proclamation that our world needs right now. It is easy to declare, "He is risen!" But if we examine our lives, there seem to be no new histories. Many people ask: "Did he really rise from the dead? Did he live again?" Where is the resurrection if no new history is visible?

I first dwell on biblical characters, and I am sure you will be able to resonate with them. From there, we will go to our daily lives, our daily experiences of the resurrection of Jesus Christ.

Biblical Characters

The Two Disciples on the Road to Emmaus

Let me start with the two disciples on the road to Emmaus (Luke 24:13–35)—two disciples. When the disciples reached their house, one of them invited Jesus to stay for a while and eat with them. According to some Bible scholars, in the custom of the time it was the woman who usually invited guests to the house. Therefore, one disciple might have been a woman.

The story begins with the very ordinary experience of frustration. The two disciples were filled with frustration and close to despair. They hoped that Jesus would be the savior, the liberator of Israel, and then he was put to death. There were even rumors that the tomb was empty. I am sure all of you have had experiences with frustration. You are frustrated with the economy, with law and order, and even with the garbage. You are frustrated with your husbands and your children. When you are frustrated, you are on the road to Emmaus. Find someone you can talk with, not necessarily someone who will advise you, but someone who will just listen.

The daily experience of frustration is the beginning of an Emmaus experience—when you walk and someone joins you, someone who looks very ordinary, a stranger. Those of us reading the Gospel know that it is the Risen Lord, someone whose mystery of resurrection we cannot fully understand. But when he comes, he comes in a very ordinary manner. He visits us in very ordinary times, in times when we fall and just want to talk about it. He comes as someone ignorant. "What are you talking about?" You pour your heart out, "Are you the only one who does not know?" The Risen Lord comes as a stranger, as someone who seems to be out of touch and does not care about what has been happening in Jerusalem. In his ignorance he tells you: "Oh, you fools. Oh, you people of little understanding. Do you really understand?" This is a question of the Risen Lord, "Do you really understand? Do you really know what is happening?"

The situation has been reversed. The stranger who looked ignorant will now reveal the disciples' lack of understanding by going to the scriptures. He will open to them the prophets, the Law of Moses, and explain to them all about himself. This stranger will open their minds and their hearts to the truth about himself. The

Risen One who is a stranger will explain to them who he *really* is—not some Bible scholar, not a topnotch theologian, not even a bishop.

The stranger stays for the breaking of bread, a symbol of sharing. The bread is broken so that it is shared; this is a domestic ritual among the Jews. The head of the family takes the bread, gives a blessing to God, praises God, and in the very act of praising God, the bread is no longer ordinary bread but becomes a symbol of God's presence, of God's love. The Risen Lord is recognized in the breaking of bread, in the sharing of the bread. The disciples realize, "It is the Lord." And then he disappears.

This is the beauty of the Emmaus experience, very ordinary and very quiet. A seemingly ignorant stranger slowly leads the disciples to knowledge and understanding. Their bitterness and frustration turn into burning hearts. "Were not our hearts burning within us?" But the moment of recognition only came when they saw an act of sharing. They saw the Lord whose life and death was all about sharing—sharing himself, sharing his life, sharing his blood. Theologians call it a "pro-existent" life. He lived *for others*. It was an intercessory life, a life on behalf of others. There was no moment when Jesus lived for himself, even the few times when he had to rest. When he saw the big crowd following, he would abandon his rest and continue teaching, for they were like sheep without a shepherd.

It is significant that after they see and recognize the Risen Lord, he disappears. But now, the disciples do not need to see with their eyes. They have already seen with their faith. The account ends in mission. The two disciples return to Jerusalem to tell the disciples there what had happened. They had seen the Lord. It is very ordinary, but a new history has been written. The Risen Lord has written a new history for these disciples—from ignorance to understanding, from frustration to hearts burning, from going home to going to mission. A new history has begun simply from this encounter with the Risen Lord.

Mary Magdalene

Let us go to another example, one of our favorites: Mary Magdalene. She is an ordinary woman, and in our way of stereotyping people, she is a woman of ill repute. In John 20:1–18 we find a moving scene where Mary Magdalene goes to the tomb with a lot of devotion and love, with a lot of motherly, sisterly, womanly courage, to visit the one who had shown her unconditional love. It was dangerous at that time because, even though Jesus had already been buried, the Jesus movement had to be stopped, and so the other disciples were still in danger. But Mary Magdalene, with all devotion, was able to surpass all fear and, for her, danger was nothing. She would go to the tomb with her oils to show once more her love for the one who had loved her. Nobody could love her, but here was one man who showed her what love meant. Where should she go to encounter the one who loved her? To the tomb, of course. There, she discovered that the tomb was empty.

Just like the two disciples on the road to Emmaus, Mary was an ordinary woman who wanted to show love and affection. She had a vision of angels. But she was so preoccupied and so frustrated at not finding the corpse of Jesus that she did not even recognize the angel. At times we are like Mary. If we are too preoccupied with so many things, we do not notice the angels before us. Mary's vision was blurred because she was looking for a corpse and she was weeping. The two angels were very good counselors, but Mary was not a good client. They had very good leading questions. "Woman, why are you weeping? Why?" In other words, "Where is that coming from? Why are you weeping?" She was being led to the root and she answered it well, "They have taken away my Lord, and I do not know where they have laid him." She knew. The angels made her realize she was looking for a corpse, a dead person.

Then Jesus appeared. Just as in the story of the two disciples on the road to Emmaus, she does not recognize him. Mary was too preoccupied with her quest and her tears to recognize Jesus. But Jesus, again like a good counselor, asks: "Woman, why are you weeping? Whom are you looking for?" Here, Mary Magdalene makes a mistake. If she had stopped and pondered—Yes, what am I looking for?—she would have come to the conclusion that she was looking for a corpse. Instead, she rushes to judgment, "Sir, if you have carried him away, tell me."

If Bernard Lonergan had been there, he probably would have said that Mary skipped a step in normal human consciousness. Instead of going from experience to understanding to judgment and then to action, she jumped from experience to judgment. Jesus was leading her to understanding. "What are you looking for? If you are looking for the dead, you will be forever frustrated. I am leading you. Your search will be useless. Pause, Mary. Pause. What are you looking for? You are looking for the dead but there is no more dead."

Again, the Lord appears like an ordinary person. You will not see in him a glorious person right away. You discover that he looks like a gardener. How does the encounter happen? In a very simple way. The Risen Lord utters "Mary." She was called again by name,

"Mary." I suppose nobody uttered the word "Mary" the way Jesus uttered it—with such sweetness, with such tenderness. That is when Mary knew. "Nobody calls me this way, only my Master." That was enough. No more long explanations. Just the word, which was a name, claiming her, "Mary." She recognized the Lord. She recognized him when he brought her back to herself with the word, her name, "Mary."

Many times we forget our names. Many times we do not even call people by name. In this encounter what Jesus said about the good shepherd and the sheep is fulfilled. He said: "I am the good shepherd. My sheep know my voice." They know the voice of the shepherd, and so they will not follow other voices. That is why we celebrate Good Shepherd Sunday within Easter. The good shepherd is the Risen Lord. Here, Mary, as a good member of the flock, recognizes the voice of her shepherd. A new history arises for the crying lady who was so anxious about finding a corpse. We now have a woman restored to herself by the Risen One who now claims her as Mary. She stops searching for a corpse because the real Person, who is truly alive, is here.

Mary also turns into a missioner, like the two disciples of Emmaus. The Risen Lord sends her, "Go to my brothers. Tell them that I will meet them. Tell them I am ascending to the Father and to your Father, to my God and your God. Tell them." She goes—no longer to weep among the tombs but to search for people who are alive. Look at her message. She does not say, "The Lord is risen." She says, "I have seen the Lord." The message comes from an experience, an encounter. It is easy to say, "Christ has died. Christ is risen. Christ will come again." It is much more difficult to say, "I have seen Christ crucified." Were you there when they crucified my Lord? Were you there when Jesus appeared in the garden as the Risen One? Can we say: "I have seen the Lord. I have seen the crucifixion"? Mary Magdalene can claim: "I have seen. I have seen."

A new history. That is why the fathers of the church called Mary Magdalene the apostle to the apostles. She was the one who brought the good news to the apostles. Some say the first apostle was a woman. Mary brought the good news of the resurrection to the apostles. She was the one who evangelized those who would be sent to the ends of the earth to be evangelizers. What a journey! From a wretched woman of ill repute, unloved, a cause of scandal, to a courageous and spirited apostle. A new history has been written from that simple encounter centered on one word, one name, "Mary."

Peter

The story occurred immediately after the miraculous catch of fish. The disciples stayed up all night but caught nothing, and the Risen Lord told them, "Cast your net into the deep." The miraculous catch happened, and there was the recognition by the disciples that Jesus lived: "It is the Lord." They recognized the Lord, and they returned to the beach where they had breakfast. Again, an ordinary event. Breakfast with fish and some bread, not a banquet at all. An ordinary meal in an ordinary place, the workplace of the fisherfolk. The place of encounter was the lake shore, the site of their daily labor and also of their daily sorrows and frustrations. There, Jesus asked Peter three times, "Simon, son of John, do you love me more than these?"

The question was not simply, "Do you love me?" Indeed, that would have been bad enough. But other words were added, and the additions made it worse, "Do you love me *more than these?*" There are many interpretations. The one I prefer is this, "Do you love me more than the love of these other disciples?" In other words, "Peter, is your love for me the greatest? If I opened the hearts of all of these disciples, will I find the greatest love for me in your heart?"

I think the context of this question is found in John 13, where Jesus told the disciples, "Where I am going you cannot go now." Jesus knew his disciples. He knew they could not follow him.

But Peter asked, "Teacher, where are you going?"

Jesus knew. "Peter, where I am going you cannot follow me now."

Peter answered, "Why can I not follow you now?" *Hindi pa tinatawag, sumasagot na* (he was not being called, but he was already answering). And he added, "I will even lay down my life for you."

It is in the same Gospel of John that Jesus says, "No one has greater love than this, to lay down one's life for one's friends."

So by saying "I will lay down my life for you," Peter was actually saying: "Master, I am your best friend. If you open our hearts you will find the greatest love in me."

But Jesus said: "Peter, will you lay down your life for me? I know you, Peter. You will deny me. You will save your life, and you will deny me."

Of course, Jesus was right.

A few chapters later they meet again. Now, the Risen Lord goes back to him, "Peter, do you really love me more than these?" A new Peter is emerging. In that first encounter, it was a Peter who was proud, a Peter who was so sure of himself. It was a Peter who was pretending to be the savior of the Savior. "I will lay down my life for you." This was the Peter before the resurrection. The events before the resurrection must have taught him a lesson in humility, a lesson in humiliation. Now, Peter could not even say, "Yes, Lord, I love you." He replied three times: "Yes, Lord. You know that I love you." Peter could no longer rely on his own knowledge of himself. He had to rely on Jesus's knowledge of him. Here, Peter is a changed person. As Jesus is risen, a new Peter is also rising. More humble, humiliated, but humbled as well. Three times Jesus tells him, "Feed my lambs, tend my sheep." A new mission is coming. A new history.

A new person with a new mission. "You will now care for my sheep. But be clear, Peter, that they are *my* sheep. I am not giving you sheep of your own. They are mine." A new portrait is being painted. Jesus is now bolder in telling him to feed his sheep. Peter will work hard, expend every effort, and remain poor. The sheep will never be his own. He will die for the sheep, but he will not own anything. He will act out of pure service. Finally, this encounter ends with the words for which Peter has been waiting a long time; it ends with the Risen Lord telling him, "Follow me."

Ordinary People

Tonight, we will be using ordinary water, ordinary voices, ordinary flowers, and ordinary children. The priests who will officiate are ordinary people. But we will be encountering heaven and eternity in those ordinary symbols, ordinary persons, and ordinary lives. We are celebrating the Easter Vigil tonight and Easter Sunday tomorrow, not in the best of times. However, our faith tells us that Jesus is truly risen. For those of you who have been following the liturgies, I hope you will be able to say: "I have seen the Lord. I have seen a bit of heaven. I have seen a bit of eternity in my ordinary time, in my ordinary life."

Now, let me alert you to the many Easter experiences in ordinary people's lives. With the two disciples on their way to Emmaus, Mary Magdalene, and Peter to guide us, let me tell you a few stories of encounters with the Risen Lord that have created resurrection experiences and new histories.

I was once invited to preside at a graduation mass. I thought it was a regular graduation at a regular school. It turned out to be the graduation ceremonies for a group of women who used to be prostitutes. They were being rehabilitated and helped to leave their old lives by a religious congregation. They underwent human, spiritual, and even technological formation so they could acquire skills. When the sisters find that they are strong enough to be sent into the world, then they have a graduation ceremony. I was presider at the mass, and instead of a homily, the graduates were asked to share their stories with the guests. One woman went to Japan and was victimized. A teenaged girl was sold by her own father to a house of prostitution. They were very depressing stories.

I will never forget the oldest woman in that group. She began by saying: "I started as a prostitute, but when I started aging, I shifted careers. I became a recruiter of prostitutes. I became prosperous. I was able to set up houses of prostitution." She sounded very aggressive, and then she said, "I don't know why I had to meet that nun." It was as if she was angry. "Why did I have to meet that nun?"

It was an ordinary event, an ordinary meeting. She paused and started crying. For the longest time, she cried, and then she said: "This evening I'm leaving for General Santos City, and I will start a house there—not to recruit prostitutes, but to rehabilitate prostitutes. And I cannot believe that now I am a different person. I will still be running houses, but a different type of house. I cannot believe it. I cannot believe it." She ran around the room hugging the sisters, the sisters I know to be ordinary women. But through them the Risen Lord appears. A new history has begun with this woman. A new hope. I think she is very good in recruiting women, and I trust that in General Santos she will be using her talent to recruit many of the prostitutes to this new school and new life.

One of my most difficult cases as a counselor was when a friend's family suffered a tragedy. My friend came to me and asked, "Where was the Lord during our pain?"

I do not know why, but I gave him the text of the two disciples on their way to Emmaus. I saw in him a person who was frustrated with Jesus, someone who put all his hopes in Jesus, and now saw those hopes crushed by evil.

The following day he told me, "Father, the Lord spoke to me."

I asked, "What did he tell you?"

And my friend said that God answered his questions by saying, "I was there, suffering with you."

I do not know whether what he said was theologically sound. But it was enough for him. A new history opened up for his whole family. Now, when I see that family, they exude peace. A new life has opened up, a new mission.

Let me close on a personal note. I was made bishop a few months ago, and I am still grappling with this new history. I am being invited to embrace this new person. When I look back at all these events, I am more and more convinced that maybe the resurrection appearance happened in a similar fashion.

I distinctly remember I was in Cebu on October 17. Antioch. Cardinal Ricardo Vidal had invited me to talk to the Visayan bishops, who were having a pastoral assembly. We were having coffee when the cardinal's secretary approached him and said, "Your Eminence, you have a phone call."

When the cardinal returned, he said to me, *"Hoy, Chito, he also wants to speak with you."*

I took the phone. It was the secretary of the nuncio.

He said, "There are some theological questions that we have to discuss."

When I met the secretary the next day, I started the conversation by asking: "Why are you always thinking of theological problems?"

Then he said, "The Holy Father wants you to become bishop of Imus."

I looked at him. He was talking, but I was not absorbing anything.

Finally, he said: "What do you have to say?"

I opened my mouth to say "This cannot be," but when I opened my mouth, no words came out. I just started crying.

Then he gave me brandy and invited me to take dinner with them. After dinner, we went back to the receiving room, and he asked again, "What do you have to say."

I said, "I want to go home."

And I went home.

I was so frustrated that evening. I was so frustrated with the church. I was so frustrated with God. I could not understand what was happening. I went to my room.

The following day I was asked to return to the nunciature. I was invited to lunch. After lunch the secretary said to me, "If you want to say no, you are free to do so. If there are serious reasons for saying no, we will appreciate your saying so. But if there are no serious reasons, then it is on your conscience."

The resurrection experience happened. In some mysterious way I heard my name called the way Mary heard her name called. I came back to my senses. I had been running around, looking for corpses, managing so many projects, but then the Risen One appeared, and I did not recognize him. I thought he was just a gardener until he called my name. I told the secretary of the nuncio, "Only in faith and for love of the church will I agree and for nothing more. Only because of faith and because of love. Only for that."

Then he turned to me and asked, "Does that mean yes?"

I said, "Yes."

Then he said, "A new history begins for you."

There are still moments when I feel that I have yet to accept fully my new history. When I visit the different *barangays,* some old people clutch my hand and

say, "Bishop, this is the first time I have seen a bishop."
"This is the first time I have held the hand of a bishop."
"Bishop, please touch my rosary." "Bishop, please touch
me. I have cancer." "Bishop, please touch my ear. I cannot hear well." "Bishop, smile at me."

A new history. The Lord is trying to make me see
that my new history may somehow help write new
histories for others. It is quite painful. The resurrection
really happens with the descent to the dead.

I know my own experience of resurrection is nothing compared to what many of you have experienced.
I am very happy on this first Easter Triduum of mine as
a bishop. It is grace upon grace. It is the outpouring of
the Spirit, which is much more than what my mind and
my heart can contain. It is a new life, a new history. I
knew that on this journey—in the ordinariness of life;
in the ordinariness of the breakfast table; in the ordinariness of Mary, Peter, the disciples on their way to
Emmaus; and all of us—only one thing matters. When
the Risen Lord appears, may we all see him. May we
all hear our names called by him in a way that nobody
else can say. May we hear our names. May we stop, and
may a new history of mission be ours. May we all be
bound together not only by the expression, "The Lord
is risen," but also, "We have seen the Lord."

Heavenly Father, how can we even thank you? The
Risen One, your Son, who continues to form us into

the sons and daughters that you deserve, appears to us. He accompanies us in our frustrations. He accompanies us when we are weeping, running around, looking for the dead. He accompanies us in our humiliations. He accompanies us in our workplaces. He accompanies us as the Risen Lord, inviting us to share in his new life so that a new history may be born for us, for our families, for our nation. We will never be able to fathom this mystery, but one thing is sure—what matters is for us to live the new histories and the new mission that the Risen One offers us. Open our hearts. Make us generous. Form in us the eagerness of Mary Magdalene. Form in us the humility of Peter. Form in us the burning hearts of the disciples on their way to Emmaus. Then maybe, even outside the Easter season, we will proclaim in word, in deed, and in mission: "We have seen the Lord. It is the Lord!"